ORWORD

This book is written from four messages preached by Roman Kauffman, so it reads differently than if it would have been written in book form. I think this message is very important for people to understand in order to live a victorious Christian life. This message cannot be applied if you're not born again.

It is very important to take God's Word for what it says and not add man's ideas to what the Bible says. Matthew 15:9 and Mark 7:7 say, *But in vain they do worship Me, teaching for doctrines the commandments of men.*

If you are not born again here are some things for you to consider:

John 3:16: *For God so loved the world, that he gave his only begotten Son, that whosoever believeth in him should not perish, but have everlasting life.*

I John 1:9: *If we confess our sins, he is faithful and just to forgive us our sins, and to cleanse us from all unrighteousness.* Vs. 10 *If we say that we have not sinned, we make him a liar, and his word is not in us.*

Ephesians 2:8-9: *For by grace are ye saved through faith; and that not of yourselves: it is the gift of God: not of works, lest any man should boast.* (See also Ephesians 2:1-13)

Romans 10:9-11: *That if thou shalt confess with thy mouth the Lord Jesus, and shalt believe in thine heart that God hath raised him from the dead, thou shalt be saved. Vs.10 For with the heart man believeth unto righteousness; and with the mouth confession is made unto salvation. Vs. 11 For the scripture saith, Whosoever believeth on him shall not be ashamed.*

A sample prayer: Lord God, I confess with my mouth the Lord Jesus Christ as Lord of my life. I agree with everything your Word says about my sins, that they are exceedingly sinful. By faith in your Word, I believe that your blood can wash away all of my sins. I believe your power within me can take away all of my desires for any sins. By faith, today I am a new creature in Christ. By faith, all of my old life has passed from me. By your power within me, I am now dead to everything Satan, the world and my flesh want to offer me. I acknowledge by the same power that I am alive to live all righteousness before You and my fellow man. By faith, I now see Jesus as my victory over the flesh, the world and Satan. I am now complete in Christ. In Jesus' name I pray.

Amen

The Faith That Overcomes

sermon by: Roman Kauffman
transcribed by: P.C. Troyer Family

ISBN 13: 978-0-9821663-0-7

ISBN 10: 0-9821663-0-3

For additional copies visit your local bookstore or contact:

Paul & Melinda Troyer
2449 W. 1000 N.
Ligonier, IN 46767

2673 Township Road 421
Sugarcreek, Ohio 44681

Carlisle Printing
OF WALNUT CREEK Ltd.

$\mathcal{T}$ABLE OF CONTENTS

CHAPTER I
OUR POSITION IN CHRIST
SPOKEN BY: ROMAN KAUFFMAN

I can say I am rejoicing to be here. Praise the Lord! Some faces I have learned to know a year or two ago. Most of you I don't know, though. I rejoice to hear how God's grace is working.

I don't think it was coincidence, but God allowed me to learn about the revival here in this area. I was contemplating on that and not realizing that in short order I was going to meet you.

I praise God this evening that God's grace is working. It reminds me of a scripture in Acts 11: 21:

And the hand of the Lord was with them: and a great number believed, and turned unto the Lord.
Verse 22: *Then tidings of these things came unto the*

ears of the church which was at Jerusalem; and they sent forth Barnabas, that he should go as far as Antioch. Verse 23: *Who, when he came, and had seen the grace of God, was glad, and exhorted them all, that with purpose of heart they would cleave unto the Lord.*

That's what I would like you to have. That with purpose of heart you would cleave unto the Lord, only the Lord. Until we learn to cleave unto the Lord we will not gain ground.

Can the grace of God be seen? Absolutely! We think of God's grace as something that happens within, invisible, and doing something within the heart. That's true, but it can be seen. When Barnabas came to Antioch he saw the grace of God and was glad.

I expect to see God's grace in your lives this week. Is that too high an expectation? I don't think so. The Bible says in John if we say that we know Him, we ought to walk as He walked. God's grace is not just a feeling or a silent, invisible witness within. A lot of God's children have a wrong concept of God's grace. Too many look at grace as deliverance from the punishment of sin. And it is. But beloved, it's so much more. It not only delivers from the punishment of sin, but it delivers from the power of sin. We have to believe that in order to be victorious. The power comes from believing that we are in Christ and Christ is within us. That's the grace of God.

First of all, what I'm going to share in these meetings is not for the person that's unrepentant. These messages are not for a person who has never been born again or is not willing to walk in all the light that God has given him. These messages are not for you if that is where you are at tonight.

These messages are for those who have been born again, but are finding yourself defeated, or without assurance. You are questioning whether you were ever saved. You're wallowing around and wondering what's happening in your life. If that fits your case, then these messages are for you. I want this clear. I've preached these messages before, and some have misunderstood them. I don't want that to happen. I want you to search the scripture as we go through these messages.

One of the greatest lack among God's children is a lack of assurance in their life. That may come as a surprise for you.

Many of us have been taught from our youth that you cannot know you're saved. We have surmounted that mountain. If we are really honest tonight, there's a lack of assurance among God's children. If it wouldn't be, then you would see more fruit in people's lives; the fruits of joy and power. You would see grace more vividly. There's a lack of assurance.

Many of God's children don't have the joy of the Lord as their strength. They've been born again, and are trying to please the Lord, but lack joy, and are constantly living in defeat. They know what repentance is all about, but they know very little about what lies beyond repentance. Much of their life is lived in self-condemnation and defeat. And they don't know how to get out of it.

If this describes you tonight I'd like to encourage you. I want you to sit through these messages and be encouraged.

Is there such a thing as beyond repentance? People go to meetings, hear convicting messages, and go home and repent, but they don't go beyond repentance. They don't know what victory is. They don't know the power that is in Christ Jesus. Some of this is due to ignorance, and some to unbelief. God's children are wallowing around in unbelief, not taking God at His word.

I'm not putting down repentance. I want that clear. We all need to repent, because we all have sinned. From time to time we need to repent again, because we failed again.

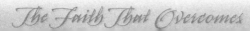
The Faith That Overcomes

Beloved, we need to go beyond that. Hebrews 6 talks about this. Not continuing to lay the foundation of repentance, but going on to perfection. Jesus talked about the one who swept his house clean by repenting, but he didn't fill it with something better. Paul told the Ephesians not to be drunk with wine, but to be filled with the Spirit.

God's children hear a lot about how to sweep their house. There's not enough teaching on what to do with a swept house. I believe God laid a burden on my heart for that. I'm talking about people that are living to the best of their knowledge, but they go to meetings and come home more burdened than when they went. Our meetings should bring an unrepentant sinner to the cross, but also encourage those that have been at the cross.

There's no life in repentance. The life and power is in what comes after repentance. The Bible doesn't say the just shall live by repentance. It says four times that the just shall live by faith.

> God's children hear a lot about how to sweep their house. There's not enough teaching on what to do with a swept house.

Repentance is part of the road that leads to justification. It doesn't produce it.

Justification by faith is very clear in Romans

chapter four. *Therefore being justified by faith we have peace with God.* (Romans chapter five). Power for the Christian is not in sweeping the house, even though that is necessary, but in the better things that you fill the house with. That's power for the Christian.

Repentance is the easy part of a Christian's life; beyond that the hard part is called the good fight of faith. Accepting forgiveness is not always easy. Accepting forgiveness and simply taking God at His Word takes a childlike faith. Simply believing and accepting it by faith.

> *R*epentance is the easy part of a Christian's life; beyond that the hard part is called the good fight of faith.

The devil has a thousand *Yea, hath God saids?* to whisper in our ears, to distract us and to keep us from going on. A person starts trying instead of trusting.

Do you know why trusting is the hardest part of a Christian's life? Because it requires going on without any tangible evidence of progress. Our five senses can't confirm that I'm a child of God. I can't feel that I'm a child of God. I can't hear that I'm a child of God. My five senses can't touch any of that. We are called to walk a life of faith that goes beyond our five senses, and that's why it's the hardest thing.

Each message has a file of its own, but they all

come under the heading of "The Faith That Overcomes." I have two requests to make from all of you before I begin. #1 *Do not judge any single message by itself.* Listen to them all before you make any conclusion.

#2 *Be a Berean.* Judge what you hear by the Word, not by any preconceived idea that you have picked up along the way. If I say something that is not scriptural, I stand to be corrected and I welcome that. I want you to know that. But don't let some preconceived idea make the scriptures say what they do not say. In other words, let the Word say what it says regardless of your experience and what you think it ought to say. Let's bow our heads in prayer.

Father, we come to You tonight in Jesus' worthy name. Lord, it's a comfort in our hearts to know He bought us, saved us, and was made sin for us that we can be made the righteousness of God in Him. He ever liveth to make intercessions for us at Your right hand. Father, that is a comfort for my soul, and I believe, Lord, that everyone tonight that has been born of the Spirit knows that comfort as well. Tonight we come to You in that name. The name of Jesus, and, Father, I come to You in childlike faith asking You to touch this place and be here tonight in the Spirit. Father, to come down upon us, Lord, and visit every heart. I plead and pray earnestly in Jesus' name, Father, that You would touch my heart and every heart here in this building. I pray, Father, for an anointing of the Holy Ghost. I pray, Father, for a mind that is clear tonight, that can understand what You say. I pray, Father, for the ability to put into words what I hear, and receptive ears that would perceive what You are saying.

Father, I pray against all powers of evil that would hinder this meeting or calm the perception of the mind, or block out what the Word says tonight. I pray against such spirits and I ask You, Lord, that You in Your power and Your presence drive such away that everyone here would have ears that can hear and hearts that can understand.

Father, magnify Yourself in these meetings. This is something we can not do. This is something the Holy Ghost must do. I'm aware tonight, Father, that without Your Spirit here, all that we are doing here is in vain. Except the Lord builds the house we labor in vain. So I invite Your presence, Lord, to bless us, and to anoint our ears. Allow this poor vessel of clay to be an instrument in Your hands tonight for Your glory and honor. I pray these things in Jesus' worthy name. Amen.

I encourage you to listen carefully; I don't want you to hear something I didn't say. A public speaker once told me, "Brother, you are not only responsible for what you say, but also for what the people hear." There's a lot of truth in that, but that is also limited, because I am aware that sometimes people hear what they want to hear, regardless what is said.

So I want to speak clearly. This is a teaching message about our sanctification. I want all Christians to get a glimpse of who we are in Christ, what we have in Christ, what our position is in Christ. The title I give this specific message is "In Christ" (even though it's under the heading: "The Faith That Overcomes").

Let's turn our Bibles to I John 5. *Whosoever believeth that Jesus is the Christ is born of God: and every one that loveth Him that begat loveth him also that is begotten of Him. By this we know that we love the children of God, when we love God and keep His commandments. For this is the love of God, that we keep His commandments: and His commandments are not grievous. For whatsoever is born of God overcometh the world: and this is the victory that overcometh the world, even our faith. 5 Who is he that overcometh the world, but he that believeth that Jesus is the Son of God? This is He that came by water and blood, even Jesus Christ; not by water only, but by water and blood. And it is the Spirit that beareth witness, because the Spirit is truth. For there are three that bear record in heaven, the Father, the Word, and the Holy Ghost: and these three are one. And there are three that bear witness in earth, the Spirit, and the water, and the blood: and these three agree in one. If we receive the witness of men, the witness of God is greater; for this is the witness of God which He hath testified of His Son.*

The Bible says: *Let God be true, but every man a liar.* In other words if you tell me something I haven't seen and I believe it, then I believe your witness. The witness of God is greater in that God cannot lie. You could have lied to me, or I could have lied to you. But remember, you will never find yourself falling if you stand on the Word!

10 He that believeth on the Son of God hath the witness in himself: he that believeth not God hath made Him a liar; because he believeth not the record that God gave of His Son. And this is the record, that God hath given to us eternal life, and this life is in His Son. He that hath the Son hath life; and he that hath not the Son of God hath not life. It's that clear. *These things have I written unto you that believe on the name of the Son of God; that ye may know that ye have eternal life, and that ye may believe on the name of the*

Son of God. And this is the confidence that we have in Him, that, if

These things have I written unto you that believe in the name of the Son of God; that ye may know that ye have eternal life,

we ask anything according to His will, He heareth us: 15 And if we know that He hear us, whatsoever we ask, we know that we have the petitions that we desired of Him. If any man see his brother sin a sin which is not unto death, he shall ask, and he shall give him life for them that sin not unto death. There is a sin unto death: I do not say that he shall pray for it. All unrighteousness is sin: and there is a sin not unto death. We know that whosoever is born of God sinneth not; but he that is begotten of God keepeth himself, and that wicked one toucheth him not. And we know that we are of God, and the whole world lieth in wickedness. 20 And we know that the Son of God is come, and hath given us an understanding, that we may know Him that is true, and we are in Him that is true, even in His Son Jesus Christ. This is the true God, and eternal life.

Let's not pass over these words lightly. Remember what the title of the message is: *"In Christ"*… We are in Him. That is true, even in His Son Jesus Christ. *This is the true God, and eternal life.*

Verse 21, *Little children, keep yourself from idols. Amen.*

Let us notice verse 4, *For whatsoever is born of God overcometh the world: and this is the victory that overcometh the world, even our faith.*

The theme of these messages is "The Faith That Overcomes." Revelation 12:11: *And they (the saints) over came him (Satan) by the blood of the Lamb and by the word of their testimony; and they loved not their lives unto the death.*

The three steps to victory, whether for the sinner to get saved or the saint who continues on faithful, take faith to experience victory.

Faith in the blood, first of all. This produces a testimony, and that takes faith to share with someone, because the Christian testifies of things unseen as yet. It takes faith not to love our lives, to believe things we can not see, and sacrifice our life for purposes that are beyond the present.

Four times the Bible says, *The just shall live by faith.* Do we know what it means to live by faith day by day, moment by moment? Why are the majority of professing Christians living defeated lives? Why can't they overcome besetting sins, bad habits, and weaknesses? Why is there not more joy among believers, when the Bible promises not only power to conquer, but to be more than conquerors? That's God's Word.

That's God's promise to us—to be more than conquerors; not just live, but have abundant life. Abundant life to live for Jesus every day, every moment.

Beloved, all the provisions are here in God's Word. We do not have to be dabbling in sin. The power is here. It's not a failure on God's part to supply what we need to live every day in victory, in joy, above sin. What's wrong? Doesn't the gospel work?

> *W*hy is there not more joy among believers, when the Bible promises not only power to conquer, but to be more than conquerors?

It works. The gospel works. We're not applying it if we're not experiencing victory. I doubt whether anyone here would say the gospel doesn't work. But is it working daily in your life? If it isn't, we are either not believing it or we are believing another gospel.

And beloved, it's very easy to get into believing another gospel. I challenge you to listen and go by the scriptures, not some preconceived ideas. When the prophet of old prophesied concerning Jesus, he said, "He—Jesus Christ—would come and save His people <u>from</u> their sins... not <u>in</u> their sins." From their sins speaks of power, not only the power to deliver the people from their past sins, but from the power of the present sins. Most professing Christians don't believe that; yes, they believe Jesus saves from the past sins, but not from the power of the present sins. They expect to sin!

For many, deliverance from present sin is a theological acknowledgment. It's something they know in their heads, but they don't believe it in a daily reality. Paul said "I am not ashamed of the gospel." Why wasn't he ashamed? Why could Paul say that?

Because he looked at the gospel message as that which delivers. The gospel works for any person, any culture, of all languages.

If you apply the gospel as it needs to be applied, you will have victory. And Paul knew that! He looked at the gospel message as a message that delivers <u>from</u> sin, not <u>in</u> sin.

Sometimes you hear a person saying, "I'm just a sinner saved by grace," and it's supposed to sound humble. That is not humility. That is nothing but unbelief. Paul said it's the power of God unto salvation. It's the power of God unto victory for everyone that believes. Paul recognized that it's the power of God that worketh in a believer's life, not some human resolution.

We're about to come to the New Year, and I wonder how many people will make resolutions. I've made many over the years. There's no power in resolutions. No. How many people have made a resolution, I'm going to stop smoking the first of January, only to fail? Some have, with the power of the flesh, overcome habits. But the motivation is not Christ.

If the gospel we believe in doesn't deliver from sin, then we are believing another gospel. The faith I'm talking about is the faith that works, it delivers, and it overcomes.

The reason behind many defeated lives is one of two things, either people don't believe the gospel message (they don't take God for what He says), or they believe another gospel. Another gospel can be as little as an accumulation of man-made ideas through reasoning around truth, and making the truth say what it doesn't say. That's all it takes to have another gospel.

Man is often tempted to interpret the gospel by his experience rather than interpreting his experience by the gospel. The gospel must be applied by faith. Sometimes the easiest answer to weak faith and simple unbelief is to make the scriptures say what they don't say. It takes an honest heart and a humble spirit to believe the gospel, especially if you have been taught wrong.

Sometimes you meet a new Christian. It's marvelous how he takes God at His Word, and then you meet a Christian of twenty years, who has rationalized and preconceived ideas of what the Word should say rather than what it does say, and this young convert goes circles around him in faith. It's simple faith.

I often wish I could read the Bible for the first time and drink it in for what it says.

My wife and I have been Christians 27 or 28 years, and I've had some questions about some of the theology or terms of speech, then God enlightened my understanding over the past few years. I've been searching, but God has opened up to me in this area of faith, and overcoming power like never before. I wrote it off as nothing more serious than terminology. Just a different way of saying the same thing, but lately I began to see it more seriously.

Yes, it can be a matter of terminology, but I believe a lot is a result of theological error. And that can lead you down a wrong path and result in defeated lives. Instead of taking God's Word at face value, people interpret it by their own experience—especially if they live in defeat.

How many people, not living victoriously, excuse their own lives by reading Romans 7? Many go to Galatians 5:17:

For the flesh lusteth against the Spirit, and the Spirit against the flesh: and these are contrary the one to the other: so that ye cannot do the things that ye would.

People totally pass by verse 16 which interprets verse 17.

They justify their lack of victory and give license to sin and defeat. I question how some look at Jeremiah 17:9: *The heart is deceitful above all things and desperately wicked. Who can know it?* Some apply this verse to a converted person.

God says in Hebrews 8:10: *I will put my laws*

> *If you don't believe that you have a new, sanctified heart, how strong is your assurance?*

into their mind, and write them in their hearts. Ezekiel 11:19: *I will put a new spirit within you; I will take the stony heart... and will give them an heart of flesh.* Ezekiel 36:26: *A new heart also will I give you, and a new spirit will I put within you.*

How can a converted person apply Jeremiah 17:9 to a converted heart?

By doubting God's promises of a new heart and interpreting it according to our own experience. If you don't believe that you have a new, sanctified heart, how strong is your assurance? How can you depend on what the Spirit says to you? Can you believe you're hearing from God if you are constantly suspicious?

The faith that overcomes—the first thing we want to address is our standing with Jesus Christ. Are you aware, if you have been truly born again, that you are in Christ Jesus? Let's look at our position in Him—where we are in Him and what that means to us. Every true Christian went through regeneration: a time in their life when they, by faith, became a new creature; from a wicked, corrupt, self-centered sinner to a humble, broken, blood-washed saint. Titus 3:3-7 describes it well.

In this regeneration experience we were redeemed, bought back by God through Christ's death. God lost His creation to the devil through Adam's sin, but bought them back through His Son's death. This is clearly written. Romans 5:19: *for as by one man's disobedience many were made sinners, so by the obedience of one shall many be made righteous.*

When Christ bought us with His own blood we became His possession. Christians, you don't own yourself...you are owned by Jesus Christ. What a blessed position! Paul reminds us in I Corinthians 6:19, 20: *You are not your own, you don't belong to yourself, for ye are bought with a price. Therefore, because of this, glorify God with your physical body and with your spirit which are God's.* We have such a close relationship with Christ that we are *in Him.*

I'm taking God at His Word. You search the Bible if you want to get blessed. Jesus talks of this in John 14:20: *At that day ye shall know that I am in my Father, and ye in me, and I in you.*

I love that verse. When I was born again, I found that verse and jumped with glee. *At that day ye shall know that I am in the Father.* I was accused of knowing that I received the Holy Spirit, and this verse tells me that at that day, I'm going to know that Jesus is in the Father and I am in Jesus and Jesus is in me.

It's an amazing thing; most of us sitting here have probably been taught all our life that you can't know you're saved, and I was taught never to read a gospel tract. I never read one before I got saved. Praise God, God can save a person that never reads a gospel tract. But I was afraid to read it. I was afraid of getting deceived, and there is nothing worse than for a person in deception being afraid of being deceived out of his deception.

This is a blessing to me: you can teach a little child, "You can not know you are saved." You can persuade him and he grows up totally convinced that you cannot know you are saved. One day he senses his sins and by the Spirit of God gets saved, and the whole world cannot tell him that he doesn't know.

That's the gospel. That's why Paul said, "I'm not ashamed of the gospel." It works!

> *There is nothing worse than for a person in deception being afraid of being deceived out of his deception.*

In II Cor. 5:17:

Therefore if any man be in Christ, he is a new creature: old things are passed away; behold, all things are become new.

II Cor. 5:21: *For He (God) hath made Him (Christ) to be sin*—listen carefully to this verse—*for He (God) hath made Him (Christ) to be sin for us, who knew no sin, that we might be made the righteousness of God in Him (in Jesus Christ).* How righteous is God? All righteous.

According to this verse, how righteous is a child of God? As righteous as God is righteous. You cannot make the scripture say anything else.

For He who knew no sin was made sin for us, so we can be made the righteousness of God, only *in Him.* As righteous as God. God's righteousness is so righteous!

If we truly believed this, how much assurance and joy would we have? How much praise? David said, "The joy of the Lord is our strength." I'm talking to a born-again child of God. He's not unrepentant, and he's not trying to hide something. He's open before God, and he'd like to have a better relationship with God.

How holy would we live if we really believed this verse? According to I John 3:3, we would purify ourselves as pure as He is. *Beloved, it doth not yet appear what we shall be.* First he starts in and he says—and I marvel at these verses—*Behold, what manner of love* the Father hath bestowed upon us, that we should be called the sons of God—manner of love simply means strange love. Behold, what strange love that God has for us that I should be called a son of God!

I'm not sure what I'm going to be like when the Lord returns. But I know this: He said, *Beloved, it doth not yet appear what we shall be, but we know that, when He shall appear, we shall be like Him.*

And then He says a strange thing—*Wer diese Hoffnung in sich hat*—*every man that has this hope within himself*—this will work such a miracle that his life will be filled with praise and joy and desire for Jesus—he will purify himself even as pure as Jesus.

Now this hope is not wishful thinking—*lebendige Hoffnung !* A lively hope! It's alive! It's real. Every man that has this expectation will purify himself even as He is pure. There is something about accepting God's love for me—it will do two things for me—it will humble me to the lowest—there's no pride involved, and it will give me the greatest desire to please only Him, out of gratitude for what He did for me.

Too many of God's children are trying to earn God's approval by what they're doing rather than out of love and gratitude for what God has done for them. Listen. Love begets love. *We love Him, be-*

cause He first loved us. I remember sitting in church and hearing this over and over again. *You shall love God with all your heart,* but I didn't know what He was going to do with me. Listen, you cannot love someone you don't trust. If you don't know where you're

> *Too many of God's children are trying to earn God's approval by what they're doing rather than out of love and gratitude for what God has done for them.*

standing with God, you're not trusting Him. You're afraid He's going to do something to you.

Love. How does love for God work in my heart? First of all I have to accept His love for me, and my response to that belief in His love will be love in my own heart for Him. And then <u>all</u> I do for Jesus will be done out of love and gratitude—a "get-to" rather than a "have-to." That's the difference between legal religion and real liberty. And that's when this book [the Bible] becomes no more a book of restriction; it becomes a book of liberation.

I remember at home the little girls would say, "Mom, do we have to do the dishes?"

"No, you don't have to if you want to." It's that simple.

A true Christian does not look at his Christian life as "what's wrong with it." His first thought is "what's right with it." The person who looks at what he can do and can't do in this life is really trying to see what he can get by with and still be a Christian. That person's life is a life of bondage instead of liberation.

Identifying with Christ, in His death and His resurrection, is by faith. That's how we become as righteous as Christ. We are justified by God through faith; justified simply means God looks at us like He looks at His Son because one day He looked at His Son as He looked at us.

Do you understand that? If I'm justified by faith, that means just as if I had not sinned. Justified means that God looks at me like He looks at His Son, because I'm now in Him—in His Son—and so He looks at me as pure as He looks at His Son. Because He looked at His Son as He looked at me with all my sins. That's what justification means.

What does it mean to identify with Christ and in His death and resurrection? In simple language it means that I, by faith, believe I died with Christ on the cross, resurrected with Him in newness of life, and am sitting with Him before God.

Oh? Is that true? You're sitting here tonight. Look how we want to interpret this by our experience.

My experience is: I am here tonight. This says I'm in

Christ Jesus. Now
how can this be?
Am I going to in-
terpret this by my

My experience is: I am here tonight. This says I'm in Christ Jesus. Now how can this be... How can Paul say, *I am crucified with Christ* when He is alive?

experience or interpret my experience by this?

How can Paul say, *I am crucified with Christ* when He is alive? By faith! By faith I believe that I died on the cross; I'm in Him; I was buried with Him; I'm resurrected with Him; and I'm sitting with Him at the right hand of the throne of God.

I found scriptures that to me were unbelievable. I gloried in them. I never saw these scriptures before. We're going to look at them. Let's look at these three steps.

According to the scripture, and <u>Listen!</u> Don't try to twist the scripture. **What you and I experience is irrelevant to what the scripture says.**

The scripture asks the question: What if some won't believe? Will their unbelief make void the faithfulness of God? God forbid! Let God and the Bible be true and every man a liar. That's what the scripture tells us.

Crucified with Christ. Do you believe that you were crucified with Christ? That the old man died

| Do you believe that you were crucified with Christ? | with Christ? That the old man is dead and gone? |

Let's go to Romans chapter 6:1-8. Let's take God's Word for what it says. Verses 1,2,3:

> *What shall we say then? Shall we continue in sin, that grace may abound? God forbid. How shall we, that are dead to sin, live any longer therein? Know ye not, that so many of us as were baptized into Jesus Christ were baptized into His death?*

Was this Bible written before you were born? You know the answer. How can the Bible say that you were baptized into Christ before you were born? How is that possible?

Just as possible as it is that Jesus Christ took sins on the cross before you were born to commit them. Verses 3-8. Verse 6, *Knowing this, that our old man* <u>is</u> *crucified*—not trying to, wanting to, or hoping that he is. That means he died with Christ; the old man is gone. Now hear me through. I want to share later what the old man is.

Is God's Word trustworthy or not? Is it dependable?

The devil is whispering in our ears, even this very moment, "Yea, hath God said?" "Hath God said this?" "If you're dead, if the old man is dead, what was it in you that made you angry yesterday? What was that?"

And immediately you use your experience to make God's Word say otherwise.

"I guess I'm not dead." That verse can't say what it appears to say. And so you continue to live a life of defeat.

Instead of reckoning yourself dead unto sin you reckon yourself alive unto it. And you'll experience enough defeat to strengthen your belief.

But Jesus told the devil that man does not live by the natural, by bread and tangible evidence—that life for victory comes from the Word that proceeds from the mouth of God. That's where life comes from.

The Word. Not some tangible evidence.

Did you ever hear someone say, "The other day the old man arose and I lost it"? I'm talking about a born-again believer.

I've heard that said many times. Is that correct theology? Does that agree with the Bible? You show me one place in the Bible where the old man arose.

One place.

The Bible deals with the old man three times and every time he's past tense. Dead.

Perhaps you're thinking, "It may not agree with the Bible, but it sure agrees with my experience." Does that change the truth? Will the truth adjust to our experience? Or will the truth pass us by and bless those who are willing to believe it and take God at His Word?

Remember, the faith that overcomes believes without seeing, needing no visible evidence. Once we have visible evidence it is no longer a walk by faith, but by sight.

There's power in believing without seeing. Jesus told Thomas: "Blessed are such that believe without seeing." They are blessed because God considers them righteous. Their faith is counted unto them for righteousness (Romans 4).

> You show me one place in the Bible where the old man arose.

Abraham's faith was counted unto him for righteousness. He believed God and therefore was called the father of faith.

Getting back to this—is it really my experience or not? In Genesis 17:5, God told Abraham that He had made him (past tense) a father of many nations before Abraham had a son.

How could God do that?

How could God say to Abraham, "I have made you a father of many nations," and he didn't have a son? He told him that before Isaac was born.

God tried his faith. As if that wasn't enough, after

Isaac was born, and Abraham saw the beginning of those many nations coming into evidence, God said, "Go kill that son Isaac."

Get rid of all the evidence! I want you to walk by faith.

How strong was Abraham's faith?

Even in all this, Abraham did not stagger. He believed God. Abraham's faith was strong enough that the logical conclusion was that God would raise Isaac from the dead! This is the faith God wants us to have. Faith without evidence. Why? *God calleth those things which be not*—there's no evidence of it—*as though they were.* But He did that with Abraham, and that was real to Abraham, and it said he had Isaac back from the dead.

Was Isaac really dead? I mean, dead. But he was dead in God's eyes. Because God counted that thing which was not, as though it was. And Abraham counted it the same and received his son back from the dead. That's Bible truth.

The Bible refers to the old man three times, and each time it's in the past. Romans 6:6, Ephesians 4:22, and Colossians 3:9. We are to reckon the old man dead. I find no scripture to support the idea that he resurrects from time to time and needs to be crucified again.

If I was crucified with Christ—Romans 6:6—that means I died with Christ. The faith that overcomes is faith in the old man being already dead—not trying to crucify him. Listen to all these messages, because there's a lot of scripture we're going to cover on it.

The old man was crucified with Christ 2,000 years ago. What other death are we to identify him with?

If you are told to go and crucify the old man again, and again, how are you going to crucify him? And what death are you supposed to reckon him already dead with, if Christ died 2,000 years ago? When a sinner comes to repentance, this truth is activated into his experience by faith. Just as Jesus took our individual sins upon Himself before they were ever even committed, so He took the old man along as well.

Romans 6:6 is very clear. Paul says in II Corinthians 5:14, *We thus judge, that if one died for all, then were all dead.*

In clearer translation Paul says, *And this is the conviction that we have arrived at: If one man died on behalf of all, then all thereby became dead men.*

If the old man is dead, what happens when a Christian falls into sin, say fornication? If it wasn't the old man that committed the sin, what was it?

Well, it was the new man, giving in to the appetites of the flesh. That's what it was.

Let me explain. The desires of the flesh are not the same as the old man. If you're starting to question this, did Adam have an old man? Did the devil have an old man? How could they sin without an old man? They sinned because of the way they were created. Every being that God created, including the angels in heaven, has the ability to go against better knowledge.

Why? They don't have an old man to contend with. But the Christian, after the new man is resurrected with Christ, still has the flesh to deal with.

The flesh and the desires of this body are not the same as the old man. Most people lump them together and then it does not make sense. How come I fell last week if the old man is dead and gone?

The old man is the body of sin, whereas appetites and desires are part of our necessary makeup. We can not live physically without these. For instance, God created us with an appetite to eat. If He would take away the appetite, we couldn't live. We'd stop eating. So the appetites we have in this physical body are not the same as the old man that was dead and buried with Christ.

> A resurrected life is a life of victory.

When these appetites go beyond what is lawful they become sin.

The same Paul that said, "I am crucified with Christ," also said, "I keep my body under." In other words, Paul recognized there's a difference between the two. He still had his body to contend with.

Paul is telling us in Romans 6:4 that if there was a death and burial, there is going to be a resurrection. A resurrected life is a life of victory.

The same power of the Spirit that brought Jesus back from the dead, the same Spirit will indwell the believer. Isn't that a comfort?

It's when these appetites go beyond what is lawful that a man falls. Paul knew the difference between the old man and the sensibilities clearly.

Paul said the old man was crucified in Galatians, dead in Romans 6, and again dead in Colossians 3, and he still had to keep his body under in Corinthians.

What happens when the Christian falls into sin? Let's read I Corinthians 6:13-20:

Meats for the belly, and the belly for meats: but God shall destroy both it and them. Now the body is not for fornication, but for the Lord; and the Lord for the body. And God hath both raised up the Lord, and will also raise up us by His power. Know ye not that your bodies are the members of Christ? Shall I then take the members of Christ, and make them the members of a harlot? God forbid. V16 What? Know ye not that he which is joined to a harlot is one body? For two, saith He, shall be one flesh. But he that is joined unto the Lord is one spirit. Flee fornication. Every sin that a man doeth is without the body; but he that committeth fornication sinneth against his own body. V19 What? Know ye not that your body is the temple of the Holy Ghost which is in you, which ye have of God, and ye are not your own? For ye are bought with a price: therefore glorify God in your body, and in your spirit, which are God's.

Verse 13: Both meats and the physical body are going to eventually pass away and go back to earth. Nevertheless, our bodies are members of Christ because we are in Him, the temple of the Holy Ghost, verse 15 & 19.

I'm talking about a Christian who commits fornication. Shall the members of Christ be joined to a harlot? In other words shall Christ be joined to a harlot? V16: *What? Know ye not that he which is joined to a harlot is one body? For two, saith He, shall be one flesh.*

When a sinner commits fornication, it's the old man with his fleshly desires that commits it, and Christ is completely out of the picture. When a Christian commits fornication, it's the new man and much more serious because he drags Christ's testimony along with it. He does not drag Christ into sin. That's not what I'm saying. Christ cannot be tempted, neither tempteth He any man—that's in James. But if a Christian sins...look what happens—what he does with Christ's name.

People look at it in a sense as Christ joined to a harlot—this man professes to be a Christian, and here he fell. See why the devil wants Christians to fall? He has ten times more leverage for the unconverted heart to stay unconverted if he can get a Christian to fall into sin like that. It's powerful to him.

The Christian's body is the temple of the Holy Ghost. Colossians 3:2: *Set your affections on things above, not on things on the earth.* Why? V 3: Because

I am dead. I'm not trying to be or wanting to be; I'm already there by faith. It says so.

I am in Christ so that my whole life is hid in Christ. That means the old man is dead and the new man is so deeply in Christ that he is hidden. God sees one new man in Christ, and that makes the Christian acceptable in the Beloved. Why is it important that we believe that we have died? Because without faith in this fact we will continue to live defeated lives.

> The one is trying to make myself acceptable to God, while the other is accepting my position in Christ.

Let me tell you why. What's the difference between trying to die daily and reckoning myself dead and crucified with Him? The one is trying to make myself acceptable to God, while the other is accepting my position in Christ. The one tries to gain confidence by experience, while the other gains experience by confidence. The one is interpreting the Word by his experience, while the other interprets his experience by the Word. The one is trying to add to the finished work, and the other is accepting the finished work. The one is trying to live for Christ, while the other is living by Christ. In short, the one is trying and the other is trusting.

Let's go to the next one, resurrected with Christ.

The Faith That Overcomes

Romans 6:3-8 again:

Know ye not, that so many of us as were baptized into Jesus Christ were baptized into His death? Therefore we are buried with Him by baptism into death: that like as Christ was raised up from the dead by the glory of the Father, even so we also should walk in newness of life. 5. For if we have been planted together in the likeness of His death, we shall be also in the likeness of His resurrection: knowing this, that our old man is crucified with Him, that the body of sin might be destroyed, that henceforth we should not serve sin. 7. For he that is dead is freed from sin. 8. Now if we be dead with Christ, we believe that we shall also live with Him.

Paul is telling us in verse 4 that if there was a death and burial there will be a resurrection. The resurrected life is a life of victory. It's a life lived in the Spirit where the power of God is one's daily life. The same power of the Spirit that brought Jesus back from the dead will indwell the believer.

> *Like as Christ was raised up from the dead by the glory of the Father, even so we also should walk in newness of life.*

How can a person live in victory? Because Christ living within is enough power that he can live above sin. *Like as Christ was raised up from the dead by the glory of the Father, even so we also should walk in newness of life.*

If you are facing difficulties and if you are wondering if God will be able to see you through, remember, the same power that raised up Jesus Christ from the dead indwells you.

What about sitting with Christ in heavenly places? You and I, whoever is in Christ both figuratively and by the authority of God's Word, have died, are buried, have resurrected, and are seated in heavenly places with Christ.

Listen to Ephesians 2:4-6: *But God, who is rich in mercy, for his great love wherewith He loved us, even when we were dead in sins*—He loved us—*hath quickened us together with Christ*—by Christ—*by grace ye are saved*—He does not stop there—*and hath raised us up together*—with Christ—*and made us sit together*—with what? With Jesus—*and made sit together in heavenly places in Christ Jesus:*

I used to read that these are heavenly places, so God raised every Christian and He's making us sit together in heavenly places. Listen, if these are heavenly places, I wonder what heavenly places are like.

That's not what he's talking about.

There is that word again—*in.* In Christ Jesus. Listen to verse 6 in another translation: *And God raised us up with Christ and through our union with Christ made us sit down with Him in heaven.*

That's what it says.

According to God's Word those who are in Christ are figuratively with Him at the right hand of God by faith.

Listen to Colossians 3:3,4: *For ye are dead, and your life is hid with Christ in God. When Christ, who is our life*—Now as I read this, remember Paul's words: *Nevertheless I live; yet not I, but Christ in me: and the life that I now live, I live by the faith of the Son of God.* So he is putting himself in with Christ.

When Christ, who is our life, shall appear, then shall ye also appear with Him in glory. In other words, Paul is saying, "You are dead and your life is so hid with Christ in God, that when Christ comes back, He's going to bring you with Him." By faith.

When Christ, whom we live in and are hid in, shall appear, shall come again, then we will be coming with Him in glory.

"I am crucified with Christ," Paul is saying, "nevertheless I am living, yet it's not the old man, it's not the old me, but Christ has taken up residence in me and the daily life I now live in this physical body, I live by the faith of the Son of God."

I want you to notice something. He does not say, "I live by the faith <u>in</u> the Son of God"—he says, "I live by the faith <u>of</u> the Son of God."

Christ's life totally engulfed Paul, and he was so hid that Christ lived His life through Paul. That's why he could say, "I live by the faith of the Son of God." Not by faith <u>in</u> the Son of God.

This is truly the faith that overcomes; nothing can withstand it. Romans 8:1: *There is therefore now no condemnation to them which are in Christ Jesus.*

I said earlier in the message, that when a Christian sins, it's different than when a sinner sins. When a Christian sins that does not put him back into the category of a sinner. It puts him back to a saint that has sinned.

Let me ask you something. A sinner has no hope. Ephesians says that we were once there—having no hope. Now you are born again, you get up in the morning and you are not feeling the best, so instead of getting up, saying, "I will rejoice and be glad in this day the Lord has made," you get up grouchy, and instead of letting God rule your life, you sass your wife off.

> He says (Paul), "I live by the faith <u>of</u> the Son of God."

You go to work. It was wrong; God knows it's wrong. You go to work and you have a wreck on the way to work and you get killed. Are you lost? Were you a sinner because you sassed off your wife? Or did you sin and you need to repent?

When your life is hid with Christ in God, it tells us in James, that sin when it is <u>finished</u> brings forth death. Finished sin is the time it takes when a man will not repent. And I can't tell you how long that time is. Because God alone knows.

But if you fail or sin, God puts His finger on that, and He asks you to repent. He gives you opportunity. You're not lost then saved, then lost then saved, then lost then saved every time you make a failure.

That's the difference between a sinner—he's lost! He's lost, because he's a sinner! But a person that is saved and sins—God gives him opportunity to repent. Eventually if he will not repent, he'll lose out. I'm not talking Calvinism. I'm not talking unconditional eternal security, beloved.

I don't believe in that.

Sin, when it is finished, bringeth forth death.

But when a Christian commits fornication, according to I Corinthians 6, it's not the old man that sins, but the new man that falls.

Christ would not be involved in the sin. This is not my persuasion at all. It's the testimony of Christ that is marred, not Christ Himself.

Nevertheless, I do not believe that the old man is come back to life each time the Christian sins. It's the new man, yielding to his physical desires and appetites. It's when he is not keeping his body under, like Paul says in I Corinthians.

This is what can happen when he doesn't reckon the old man dead, and himself dead unto sin and alive unto God (Romans 6). Or when he forgets that he was purged from his old sins (II Peter 1).

We need to understand that there's a difference between the old man who's a sinner and the appetites and desires a Christian still has to live with.

Again we could go back and read Romans 6 verses 5-7 for clarification on this.

For if we have been planted together in the likeness of His death, we shall be also in the likeness of His resurrection: Knowing this, that our old man is crucified with Him, that the body of sin might be destroyed, that henceforth we should not serve sin. For he that is dead is freed from sin.

Paul says in verse 6 that when Christ was crucified, the old man was crucified with Him, and this is what destroyed the body of sin, and from then on, He says from henceforth, we should not serve sin.

Nowhere in the Bible do I find scripture that the old man rises from time to time and the Christian is called to put him to death again. I don't find any scripture to support that theory, though it is very strong among some of God's children.

> We need to understand that there's a difference between the old man who's a sinner and the appetites and desires a Christian still has to live with.

Reckon ourselves to be dead indeed unto sin, and alive unto God.

Let's look at that word, reckon. The word indeed first of all means sure. We are supposed to reckon him dead for sure. Indeed. Dead for sure.

Reckoning does not create reality. I want you to remember this. Reckoning does not create reality. A lot of people read this and think, "I'm going to have to put the old man to death—because I'm supposed to reckon him dead."

How can you put something to death that you are supposed to figure dead already? It doesn't make sense.

Reckoning <u>reflects</u> upon the reality that God has already spoken. In other words, you don't make things happen by reckoning. Reckoning is accepting what has already happened and taking God at His Word. And then interpreting God's Word through our experience.

Let's look at what Paul calls the body of sin, that was destroyed at the death of Christ. The body of sin, I believe, is the natural Adam, that inherited natural gravitation towards sin. This is the body of sin that each one of us has received from Adam.

Let me illustrate this.

When you recall before you were born again, you naturally had a gravitation towards things that were wrong. Naturally. You gravitate towards them.

I remember as a carnal man, I loved dirty jokes. When I got born again, I hated them with a passion. To this day I still hate them.

What happened? The old man was crucified.

Now I could still go back and do things that were wrong. I'm born again and when I hear a dirty joke the natural thing is to hate it and get away from it. Why? Christ is in me and Christ and sin don't mix.

You might have been into pornography. If you truly experienced salvation, there's something within you that repels against that. Oh, you might look at something again out of curiosity—but the natural thing that rises within you immediately after you've been born again is—what is it? It's the Spirit of God within you.

The old Adam was crucified back with Christ. And when you were saved, you accepted that by faith and activated it into your experience, just like the forgiveness of your sins.

Read Romans 5:12-19: *Wherefore, as by one man sin entered into the world, and death by sin; and so death passed upon all men, for that all have sinned:* Vs. 13 *(For until the law sin was in the world: but sin is not imputed when there is no law.* Vs. 14 *Nevertheless death reigned from Adam to Moses, even over them that had not sinned after the similitude of Adam's transgression, who is the figure of Him that was to come.* Vs. 15 *But not as the offence, so also is the free gift. For if through the offence of one many be dead, much more the grace of God, and the gift by grace, which is by one man, Jesus Christ, hath abounded unto many.* Vs. 16 *And not as it was by one that sinned, so is the gift: for the judgment was by one to condemnation, but the free gift is of many offences unto justification.* Vs. 17 *For if by one man's offence death reigned by one; much more they which receive abundance of grace and of the gift of righteousness shall reign in life by one, Jesus Christ.)*

Vs. 18 *Therefore as by the offence of one judgment came upon all men to condemnation; even so by the righteousness of one the free gift came upon all men unto justification of life.* Vs. 19 *For as by one man's disobedience many were made sinners, so by the obedience of one shall many be made righteous.*

They are all very clear.

When the old man is by faith crucified with Christ, it's a death blow towards the natural gravitation towards sin.

It's not that the Christian cannot sin. I know there are people teaching that once a person is born again he cannot sin again. And if he does sin, it's because he has never really been born again.

I don't believe that.

No, but at the same time I believe that a Christian can live above sin. Christ would not ask us to live a life of holiness if He did not make it possible.

A new spirit, a new heart is given to the Christian. The natural gravitation to sin is gone.

He can still fall into sin. With his physical body and makeup, he still has to fight the good fight of faith. A Christian still has the physical flesh with its desires and appetites to deal with.

Romans 8:13 says, *For if ye live after the flesh, ye*

shall die: but if ye through the Spirit do mortify the deeds of the body, ye shall live.

How do we through the Spirit mortify the deeds of the body? How does this take place?

By reckoning the old man dead and the new man resurrected with Christ in the newness of life. This is a deliberate choice that we make.

In your Christian life you will not rise above what you believe.

If you believe you're just a sinner saved by grace, you're going to live like a sinner that's trying to live by grace.

We tend to interpret the Bible according to our experience. We make the Bible fit our experience instead of accepting God's Word for what it says, but our feelings and our experiences don't determine reality or duty.

> ...I believe that a Christian can live above sin.

In closing let's turn to Romans 5:1-2. *Therefore being justified by faith, we have peace with God through our Lord Jesus Christ: By whom also we have access by faith into this grace wherein we stand, and rejoice in hope of the glory of God.*

> In your Christian life you will not rise above what you believe.

Paul says through Jesus we have access by faith into this grace wherein we stand. Now stop right there!

It's a position. We have access—because of Jesus Christ—we have access into this grace wherein we stand.

We have taken up this position in Christ. We stand there, not budging, regardless what my experience is or what my emotions are trying to tell me tonight. I <u>stand</u> on God's Word, by faith.

I think of the songwriter:

> *When darkness seems to veil His face,*
> *I rest on His unchanging grace;*
> *In every high and stormy gale,*
> *My anchor holds within the vale.*
>
> *On Christ, the Solid Rock, I stand;*
> *All other ground is sinking sand.*

May God be praised.

I'm going to ask James Schmuckers to sing a song. In closing we'll sing that song. That song fits perfectly what I'm trying to say.

Song:

I am crucified with Christ, nevertheless I live,
Yet not I, but Christ liveth in me,
And the life which I now live in the flesh,
I live by the faith of the Son of God,
Who loved me and He gave Himself for me.

Who loved me. Who loved me. Who loved me
And He gave Himself for me.
Who loved me. Who loved me. Who loved me
And He gave Himself for me.

If ye then be risen with Christ,
Seek those things which are above,
Where Christ sitteth on the right hand of God.
Set your affections on things above,
Not on things of the earth;
Ye are dead and your life is hid with Christ in God.

Ye are dead, Ye are dead, Ye are dead
And your life is hid with Christ in God.
Ye are dead, Ye are dead, Ye are dead
And your life is hid with Christ in God.

Let's bow our heads.

Thank You, Father. Thank You for Your Word. I pray, dear God, that if no other impression was made in our hearts tonight other than that we take You at Your Word, accept it for what it says, regardless of our experience, or emotions, then God be praised.

Dismiss us with Your blessing. I pray in Jesus' name. *Amen*

Again I'd like to greet each one in Jesus' worthy name this evening.

I'm glad to be here. I'm here with anticipation; I trust you are too. The Lord is good, merciful as we trust and rest in Him daily to supply our every need and give us clear direction. I trust you have been praying.

I think of the song, "I need Thee every hour. I need Thee, oh, I need Thee."

These messages come under the theme of "The Faith That Overcomes."

I'll remind you that these messages are meant for the child of God—they're not for the sinner, to put a pillow under his head or bring him comfort when he is in rebellion.

These messages are for the person that is walking in all the light that he has, but he doesn't know the Way. Many of God's children today (and I can identify with this myself) lack assurance. They don't realize it, but a lot of their problem is <u>simple</u> unbelief.

They are wanting to accomplish something that God has already accomplished. That's one of the saddest things: a person in unbelief and doesn't know it. When God says something in His Word, and instead of simply taking it with childlike faith (that's what God means), they try to do it.

And they don't get anywhere. They are waiting on God, while God is waiting on them to accept what He has already done. And it's simply not taking God at His Word. That is my thrust, this weekend, to bring out scriptures—because the faith that overcomes is not a once and for all thing.

It's a continual fight, because it believes in something that has no tangible evidence to prove it.

So we are constantly bombarded by the devil. "Yea, hath God said?"

We get second thoughts; we start reasoning around God's Word, instead of simply taking it for what it says, and we end up with confusion.

God's Word says what it means and means what

it says. The sooner we understand that and take it for what it says the better off we are.

We're going to go over a bit of what we shared last night, realizing that there are a lot of things we need to be reminded of.

I talked about the importance of reckoning who and what the person is "in Christ." And that if he is truly born again and walking with God, he is "in Jesus Christ." He's part of the Godhead, by faith.

And about the swept house, and how it's just as important to know when to stop sweeping and go from there, etc.

And one of those seven worse devils that can enter into the empty house, that is worse than unbelief and is harder to get rid of, is a self-righteous attitude. You start with religion without a relationship with Jesus and end up with a self-righteous attitude like the Pharisees had.

I talked about the old man being dead and crucified with Christ and the importance of exercising faith in this fact, etc., and what this will do to your everyday life if you really accept that for what it says.

You should always interpret your experience by what the Bible says, and never interpret the Bible by your experience.

We have to go by the Word. Stand on it. Through Jesus Christ we have access into this faith wherein we stand. We stand firm on that. Solid. On that Rock.

I'd like to continue and share another message with the same theme: "The Faith That Overcomes." But the title will be "The Out-living of the In-living."

Instead of primarily focusing on who the Christian is in Christ by faith, I want to share how the faith that overcomes gives power over the power of sin in our daily lives.

> You should always interpret your experience by what the Bible says, and never interpret the Bible by your experience.

The scripture in John: *This is the victory that overcometh, even our faith.* Have you spent time thinking about that verse? Before these meetings?

I have.

I've spent a lot of time thinking about them. Because I realized that I needed victory over the world and it talks about a <u>faith</u> that overcomes the world.

It's not talking about a certain way of life, or about positive thinking. It's about standing in this place with Christ Jesus.

That's what the faith that overcomes is all about. It is accepting the position in Jesus Christ that God says that I have. And standing on that regardless how I feel. That's the faith that overcomes.

The faith that gives you power. The faith that brings joy to your life. The faith that brings victory in the time of temptation.

It's the faith of what you are in Jesus Christ. *And this is the victory that overcometh the world, even our faith* (I John 5:4).

This evening I want to talk about living this faith. The out-living of the in-living faith. Let's read Romans 8:1-14. Verse 1:

> *There is therefore now no condemnation to them which are in Christ Jesus, who walk not after the flesh, but after the Spirit.*
>
> *2 For the law of the Spirit of life in Christ Jesus hath made me free from the law of sin and death.*
>
> *3 For what the law could not do, in that it was weak through the flesh, God sending His own Son in the likeness of sinful flesh, and for sin, condemned sin in the flesh:*
>
> *4 That the righteousness of the law might be fulfilled in us, who walk not after the flesh, but after the Spirit.*
>
> *5 For they that are after the flesh do mind the things of the flesh; but they that are after the Spirit*

> *For as many as are led by the Spirit of God, they are the sons of God.*

the things of the Spirit.

6 For to be carnally minded is death; but to be spiritually minded is life and peace.

7 Because the carnal mind is enmity against God: for it is not subject to the law of God, neither indeed can be.

8 So then they that are in the flesh cannot please God.

9 But ye are not in the flesh, but in the Spirit, if so be that the Spirit of God dwell in you. Now if any man have not the Spirit of Christ, he is none of His.

But ye are not in the flesh, but in the Spirit—he simply says ye are not. He's talking to Christians.

10 And if Christ be in you, the body is dead because of sin; but the Spirit is life because of righteousness.

11 But if the Spirit of Him that raised up Jesus from the dead dwell in you, He that raised up Christ from the dead shall also quicken your mortal bodies by His Spirit that dwelleth in you.

12 Therefore, brethren,—because of this—*we are debtors, not to the flesh, to live after the flesh.*

13 For if ye live after the flesh, ye shall die: but if ye through the Spirit do mortify the deeds of the body, ye shall live. It's that clear.

14 For as many as are led by the Spirit of God, they are the sons of God.

Let's bow our heads and pray. Father, we come to You again in Jesus' name. First of all to thank You, Father, for Your Word, and to thank You that we have this liberty here in this country, the freedom to come together as we will, and share what the Word means and what the Holy Spirit has taught us. Father, we truly are a blessed people. May we not use this blessing and Your grace as an occasion of the flesh to succeed in us.

But Father, may we again be reminded that You have called us for such a time as this, to lead this generation in the way of truth.

Father, I thank You for everyone that was able to come out tonight, and I pray that You would bless those who were not able to come.

I pray, Father, that You would open up the windows of heaven and pour out a blessing, Lord. A blessing that we cannot contain; that our cup would be full. It would flow through our lives and touch the lives of others, Lord.

Do it in our hearts tonight. Fill us with the Holy Spirit. Show us what Your Word really, truly means.

I pray, Father, that You would give us ears that

can hear and hearts that can comprehend and under-stand what the Spirit says, Lord. Take away our own preconceived ideas, Father, and allow the Holy Spirit to give us Your ideas, and Your concept of what the Word means.

Father, I praise You for what You have done for us. I praise You for the in-living life. I praise You for the quickening Spirit, Lord, that raised Jesus Christ from the dead and has quickened our mortal bodies. Father, in the midst of a crooked and perverse gen-eration, we can still live a life that is pleasing to You.

Yet, Father, we are still in this body, and we need to have that power continually dwelling within us and surging through our very being.

Father, moment by moment, we need You. Lord Jesus, we need You. We commit this meeting into Your hands again, Father, asking You, Lord, to do what will bring honor and glory to You and that which will strengthen Your children.

In Jesus' name. Amen.

Looking at this scripture, that the law of the Spirit of life in Christ Jesus hath made me free—hath made me free from the law of sin and death.

Now usually we tend to associate law with death, not life. That's our tendency.

But Paul says, "There is a law of life, as well as a law of death." We find this law of life is even more powerful than the law of death.

Even as light overwhelms darkness in the natural. Walk into a dark room...flip a switch—darkness has to go. When the light bulb comes on, the darkness cannot abide.

Look. There's a physical law of electricity. When light comes on, darkness has to go. That's one of the physical laws in everyday life.

There are spiritual laws as well. What is this law of life? First of all, law is an established principle that we cannot change. I'm blessed that truth is truth. Whether you or I support it, or none of us support it, truth will be truth. It stands on its own two legs. Truth is Jesus Christ Himself.

You can't take a drop of truth and put it in an ocean and it's diluted. That drop of truth will be as strong whether it's in an ocean or not. Truth is truth. Your unbelief will not make it any weaker, nor will your believing make it any stronger. It stands by itself.

Law is an established, ongoing, effective principle. It is forever settled in heaven. Though heaven and earth pass away, truth will remain and the law of the Spirit of Christ Jesus sets us free from the law of sin

> The law of life overcomes the law of sin and death just as light does darkness.

and death. Romans 8:2 is the established principle working effectively in all who are in Christ Jesus and setting them free from the power of sin and death.

The law of life overcomes the law of sin and death just as light does darkness. If you apply some of these established principles to some doctrines that are out there, it tears them to shreds. For instance, a principle God has ordained, the law of cause and effect. For every cause there's an effect behind it.

Friends, you have a law of gravity. That law of gravity is forever true and it continues to work. You cannot get rid of it. The only way that you can overcome the law of gravity is by bringing another law in that is greater. For instance, an airplane. You can strap yourself fast, and get the pilot to rev the engines. He can do all he wants to; that jet will not lift off the ground because a law of gravity holds it there.

But he can get those propellers moving and go down the runway and the law of gravity will hold it down on the ground until he brings in another law—the law of air dynamics. It doesn't put away the law of gravity, but overrides it. And that's what makes the jet take off.

The Faith That Overcomes

Now you're up in the sky a mile and you turn off the engines. Is the law of gravity still good? We all know, that jet will come down.

Well, there are established principles in God's Word.

There's a lot of talk that once you're a Christian and living in grace, the law of sin and death has no more power. The law of sin and death is as alive as the law of gravity. The only thing that supercedes the law of sin and death is the law of life in Christ Jesus who sets us free. But listen! You shut that engine off or you get to the place where you neglect God's Word, or you go through life taking interest in other things, and God's Spirit will prick your mind.

You go on in that direction where you're no longer drawing sap from the true vine. And the branch withereth. Why does the branch wither? Because the law of sin and death is in effect, like an engine that's shut off. That's why the Bible says: *Keep thy heart with all diligence; for out of it are the issues of life.*

That's why we have warnings all through the Bible, that we have to continue in Christ Jesus, to have that faith that overcomes continually—that faith that I am in Christ Jesus. And let's remember what Peter says about being purged.

Romans 8:3: *For what the law could not do, in that it was weak through the flesh...* This is not talking about the law containing ordinances, all the dos and don'ts of the commandments.

Jesus Christ condemned sin. How did Jesus Christ condemn sin? By living above sin.

How do we know that sin is condemned? Because

> Every Christian that is walking in victory in his daily life is establishing the law.

God sent His Son to live a victorious life above sin, and that it simply says He condemned sin in the flesh.

If Jesus Christ could not have lived above the reproach of sin, then no one could have been condemned for sin. But He did, and that brought condemnation upon all mankind.

Because Jesus lived without sin, He established the righteousness of the law. That I just read. Now look at verse 4: *That the righteousness of the law might be fulfilled in us, who walk not after the flesh, but after the Spirit.*

Every Christian that is walking in victory in his daily life is establishing the law. His victorious daily Christian life is saying that sin is wrong. That's what that whole verse means.

The out-living of the in-living Christ; walking in the Spirit confirms the rightness of the law. Now how is this going to be a reality in our lives?

By the faith that overcomes the world.

I want one thing clear: the faith that overcomes is not this thought of just gritting my teeth and pulling myself up by my own bootstraps.

No, no, no, don't get that idea. Through these four messages, the purpose is to get the Christian to focus on the right thing, and that is Jesus Christ.

Listen to Paul's testimony in Galatians 2:20. *I am crucified with Christ: nevertheless I live; yet not I, but Christ liveth in me: and the life which I now live in the flesh I live by the faith of the Son of God, who loved me and gave Himself for me.*

Not faith <u>in</u> God's Son…the faith <u>of</u> God's Son. That's the wording.

What's he talking about?

The person that is really in Jesus Christ is living by the power of Christ. He is living by the very faith that Jesus lived by. Paul simply says: *The life which I now live in the flesh I live by the faith of the Son of God, who loved me and gave Himself for me.*

To overcome, two aspects of faith must be our experience. Two areas where I must continually exercise faith. This is the good fight of faith.

#1: That I am dead. Crucified with Christ. That's

the number one. I'm not saying one is more important than the other. #2: That Christ lives within me.

Those two things are the hardest things for you to fight for. There's nothing harder. Those two things are the fight of faith. It's not some kind of lifestyle; it's not trying to keep your head above water when things go wrong.

> There's a difference in feeling my way into believing or believing my way into feeling.

The one is: You are continually fighting the fact that you are dead. Because there is much tangible evidence that you are not.

And God says, "Don't go by your experience. Go by what I am telling you, and your experience will fall into place."

The other one is: Christ lives in me. Well, I don't feel like Christ lives in me today.

It doesn't matter.

We have to remember there's a difference in feeling my way into believing or believing my way into feeling. It's a big difference.

Faith in these two established facts is what overcomes the world. Without faith in these, there would be no victorious Christian life.

To live victorious lives is vital importance to identify with Christ in His death, in His burial, in His ascension.

Unless we by faith make this a daily experience, Christ will be a far-off part of the Godhead that we're trying to get close to by whatever the flesh and self has to offer.

Unless we believe this we'll continually be trying to pump ourselves up or pulling ourselves up by our own bootstraps. Trying to get close to Christ with whatever the flesh has to offer.

In our relationship to Christ, we by faith must believe. We are not just brought near to Him, but into Him, no longer twain but one flesh.

We know the book of Romans is a gospel of itself. It proves how man is sinful, and the Jew is no better than the Gentile; there's none better than the other.

We all have sinned and come short of the glory of God, and because of unthankfulness (in chapter 1) God gave man over to a reprobate mind, and the steps of the degenerate.

We go to chapter 2. The Jew is no better than the Gentile. Chapter 3… All have sinned. In the latter part of chapter 3 he brings us out of that into faith and he proves that justification comes through faith. In chapter 8: There is now no condemnation in Christ Jesus. Then he goes on.

The book of Romans is designed. It puts new dimension to what I'm sharing. I don't know if Paul knew it when he wrote it or not. (I'm not sure how much David was aware of the things he wrote. Maybe later he recognized it when he read it—there is a thought that he never had when he wrote it.)

Notice the way Paul started and the pivoting chapter in the Christian life is Romans 6. Do you believe that? The whole Christian life hinges on what you're doing with chapter 6. If you don't know what chapter 6 means by experimental knowledge, then you don't know what the Christian life is.

But Paul prepares the mind to accept chapter 6.

The majority of Christians do not accept chapter 6. They don't. Then they wonder why they are in chapter 7 in their daily life. They'd like to live in chapter 8, but Romans 7 is their experience.

It is because they've never really accepted chapter 6. What I mean by accepted is that they never really took it for what it says.

But Paul, in his writing of Romans, prepares the heart, step by step, until he comes to Romans 6. Paul comes in before chapter 6 and says God sees those things that be not as though they were. He is preparing the heart to believe without seeing. To believe without any tangible evidence.

He talks about Abraham and how Abraham walked by faith. I shared with you last night how God told Abraham that he was the father of many nations before he had a son.

How can God tell a person—say, young Abraham, a married man, but has no children, and God told him one day, "I have made you a father."

"A father? I don't have any children."

"That's beside the point," God says. "I have made you a father, because I look at those things that be not as though they were."

That's what Paul is trying to prepare our hearts for. So when we get to chapter 6, we can accept it for what it says. And we have people who can not see it in chapter 6. The Bible says ye are dead.

"I'm not dead. I know I'm not, because of my experience."

That's beside the point. God's Word still says what it says.

Abraham could have said, "That's not right."

> When God says it, that's the way it is. It doesn't matter whether you believe it or not.

But Abraham could have sat at the city gate, or down at the local country store, and a bunch of men would have gathered with him, talking about their children and grandchildren.

Abraham sat there without a child. He'd laugh and say, "You know what? I have more children than any of you."

"What? Come on, Abraham. You don't even have a child."

"I have more children than any of you."

"But how can you say that?"

"Because God says I have."

That's all we need. When God says it, that's the way it is. It doesn't matter whether you believe it or not. *Let God be true, but every man a liar.* That's the faith that overcomes.

If you are going to wait until you experience everything your eyes can see, you are not walking by faith. *The just shall live by faith!* The life is in faith in Jesus Christ. The faith that overcomes.

CHAPTER V

THE OUT-LIVING OF THE IN-LIVING

Let's look at this in a more practical way.

Most Christians think of overcoming sin by striving and pursuing. I know. I've experienced that in my life. That's not the way to go.

I don't have any problem if you're striving onward like the songwriter says, "Striving onward and upward." I don't have any problem if you call that striving if you're talking about exercising faith in Christ.

But most Christians think of sanctification as an ongoing maturing process, resulting from diligently pursuing Christian virtues. They try to bring about a holy life. But sanctification and holiness and power in one's life is the result of trusting, <u>not trying</u>.

Instead of trusting in facts, they try to produce the facts.

How many of us, like we read in II Peter chapter 1, add to your faith, virtue, knowledge, patience, godliness,

> But sanctification and holiness and power in one's life is the result of trusting, <u>not trying</u>.

brotherly kindness—see those things lacking in our life, so we try to produce it.

No. That's putting the horse at the wrong end of the cart.

Let's go to II Peter 1 verse 2 through 10.

Verse 2 *Grace and peace be multiplied unto you through the knowledge of God, and of Jesus our Lord,*

3 According as His divine power hath given unto us all things that pertain unto life and godliness, through the knowledge of Him that hath called us to glory and virtue:

4 Whereby are given unto us exceeding great and precious promises: that by these ye might be partakers of the divine nature, having escaped the corruption that is in the world through lust.

5 And beside this, giving all diligence, add to your faith virtue; and to virtue knowledge;

6 And to knowledge temperance; and to temperance patience; and to patience godliness;

7 And to godliness brotherly kindness; and to brotherly kindness charity.

8 For if these things be in you, and abound, they make you that ye shall neither be barren nor unfruitful in the knowledge of our Lord Jesus Christ.

9 But he that lacketh these things is blind, and cannot see afar off, and hath forgotten that he was purged from his old sins.

10 Wherefore the rather, brethren, give diligence to make your calling and election sure: for if ye do these things, ye shall never fall:

We are changed by accepting and committing our lives to these promises.

Let us look at God's Word and accept these exceeding great and precious promises—and by the way, until you commit yourself to a promise of God, you have not accepted it.

You know it. But you don't believe it. Once you commit yourself to something, then you believe it.

This Book is alive! Not this literal Book, but what it says is alive. It's Jesus Christ! *I am the Way, the Truth, and the Life.* This is the truth, but there is life in these promises once a person commits himself.

People say, "What is the new birth?" The new birth is simply what happens to a person's heart, life, and his very nature when he accepts these promises. He is transformed by the power in these promises.

And what happens? He instantly receives power that he can live above the corruption that is in the world through lust.

Now we have power in our life. I don't want to lose you; follow me along on this. A precious truth is here: God's Word.

We have power in our lives because we accepted these promises. We are changed…a new creature in Christ. *Old things are passed away; behold, all things are become new.*

Promises in God's Word, like John 3:16 and I John 1:9—we accepted these and the life of these promises became part of us.

> *And what happens? He instantly receives power that he can live above the corruption that is in the world through lust.*

Most Christians don't have a problem accepting this truth, they know they are saved by grace through faith. But where most run into a problem is verse 5—adding to their faith virtue.

Christian virtues. In other words, Christian growth. Maturing in their Christian life. When it comes to adding to their faith Christian virtues like temperance, patience, godliness, brotherly kindness, and charity, they think they have to somehow manufacture these.

They quit trusting and begin trying. They are like Abraham not trusting God with Sarah, but incorporating Hagar. And it's of the flesh.

Look at verse 9. If one lacks these virtues, it's not because he didn't try hard enough. He lacks trust. He has forgotten that he was purged from his old sins. And now he's blind and cannot see afar off. He's lost his discernment that he once had.

Look at verse 10. *Wherefore the rather, brethren, give diligence to make your calling and election sure: for if ye do these things, ye shall never fall.*

What is our calling and election?

In short, it's our salvation and our standing with God. How are we to give diligence to make this sure? Is it by pursuing Christian virtues?

No! We don't pursue Christian virtues. Christian virtues come by trusting facts, not trying to manufacture some venturous Christian life.

As we trust the facts, the virtues will sprint forth, because they are the effect of a greater cause: trust in Jesus Christ.

What facts?

The fact that I am accepted in the beloved. I have died with Him, was buried with Him, resurrected with Him. And now live in Him.

Let me illustrate. Suppose you're having a trying day. Everything is going wrong. You're weary and the tempter is trying you continually, all through the day.

> Christian virtues come by trusting facts, not trying to manufacture some venturous Christian life.

Then all of a sudden something happens and it's the last straw.

Anger wants to well up.

You've got a decision to make. You could either try to suppress the anger and at least keep it from exposing itself, but God sees the heart. Or you could just look at the facts of God's Word. When the devil tempts you, you can simply tell him, "I am dead. I am crucified with Christ and the life that I now live, I live by the faith of the Son of God, who loved me and gave Himself for me."

That's the faith that overcomes the world. God sees the heart. You can have all the determination you want. Or you can remember that the old man is dead and that you are in Christ by faith, and you have been purged from your old sins.

The one at best will suppress and keep the anger

bottled up, with no power to get rid of it, but the other will mellow you to the point where the issue isn't important enough to get angry. The one brings conviction, the other peace, joy, and the Holy Ghost.

Remember: Christ's humility brought our salvation. Our salvation brings us humility.

Many Christians are living defeated lives, not because they don't care, or because they've given up. It's not because they're no longer trying.

They read book after book on self-helps. Do this and this and you'll have victory. It's a lot simpler than that.

Believe this and you'll have victory.

It's just that simple.

But you know. There aren't too many books you can get at a bookstore and go home and read that the devil will be right at your ear and say, "Yea, hath God said?"

But try this, and you'll have him at every turn, telling you, "That's not really true. You know you're not experiencing it. That's not really true."

Many people are convicted. They can't seem to help themselves, because they lack the life and power that God gives, since they don't walk by faith. Their lives are a continual Romans 7 experience.

That which they do, their conscience does not allow, and that which they want to do, they don't get done, and that they hate, that they do (Romans 7:15). *For the good that they would do they do not. But the evil which they would not, that they do (Verse 19).*

They longingly read chapter 8… Live in the Spirit. They realize that something is drastically wrong with their life.

Then someone who is in the same shoes points out Galatians 5:17 to comfort them. *For the flesh lusteth against the Spirit, and the Spirit against the flesh: and these are contrary one to another: so that ye cannot do the things that ye would.*

That fits me. That's what that must mean. Instead of interpreting their experience by God's Word, they interpret God's Word by their experience.

But this verse is not saying, because the flesh lusteth against the Spirit, and the Spirit against the flesh, that you just can't help yourself and therefore are a slave to sin.

That's not what it means. How could that be when Romans 6:14 says: *For sin shall not have dominion over you.*

And verse 7: *He that is dead is freed from sin.*

How can that be? It doesn't jibe.

This verse must be interpreted in light of what Galatians 5:16

> Galatians 5:16: *This I say then, Walk in the Spirit, and ye shall not fulfill the lust of the flesh.*

says. The word "For" in verse 17 connects it to verse 16: *This I say then, Walk in the Spirit, and ye shall not fulfill the lust of the flesh.*

For because of that truth, verse 17 says: *The flesh lusteth against the Spirit, and the Spirit against the flesh.*

Paul is saying the total opposite. He's saying, "Walk in the Spirit and you will not fall for the things of the flesh."

Why?

Because the two don't mix. They are contrary one to the other.

Romans 8:13 says: *For if ye live after the flesh, ye shall die: but if ye through the Spirit do mortify the deeds of the body, ye shall live.*

Now a lot of people have looked at this and have recognized that a lot of fleshly things are going on in their life, so they decide: we have to put away this thing—we have to mortify the deeds of the flesh.

How do you mortify the deeds of the flesh?

The Bible says through the Spirit. Through the Spirit of the law of life in Christ Jesus that sets us free from the law of sin and death. That's how it's done.

It's the power of the divine nature, given to us as we by faith commit ourselves to God's established promises. And just believe them.

Not until those who live defeated lives in Romans 7 by faith accept Romans 6 for their answer, will they experience life in the Spirit of Romans 8.

Romans 6 is the answer for anyone who wants to experience Romans 8. It's the answer. Believe it.

We're going to turn to Romans 6 to refresh our minds.

How can a person experience total victory from day to day? How can we rise above the defeated lives many are experiencing? How does a person overcome anger? How does a Christian overcome depression? Discouragement, lust, and every other besetting sin.

Where is the power to say no to temptation?

It's all found in Romans 6, if we accept by faith what it tells us.

Let's read Romans 6:1-14.

1 What shall we say then? Shall we continue in sin, that grace may abound?

2 God forbid. How shall we, that are dead to sin, live any longer therein?

3 Know ye not, that so many of us as were baptized into Jesus Christ were baptized into His death?

4 Therefore we are buried with Him by baptism into death: that like as Christ was raised up from the dead by the glory of the Father, even so we also should walk in newness of life.

5 For if we have been planted together in the likeness of His death, we shall be also in the likeness of His resurrection:

I'd like to bring your attention to a word there. The word planted means conjoined. Do you know what the word conjoined means?

That's what Siamese twins are. Doesn't a light go on in your mind?

What are Siamese twins? I had a picture in my Bible for a long time to show people of two little girls that were Siamese twins. They had one body. They had two heads, two arms, and two legs. Their body was joined in the middle, conjoined. That's what we are in Christ.

For if we have been conjoined to Christ, in the likeness of His death, we shall also be in the likeness of His resurrection. Isn't that sweet? What a blessing.

You know, if you are born again tonight, you are a Siamese twin with Jesus Christ.

6 Knowing this, that our old man is crucified with Him, that the body of sin might be destroyed,

> *Romans 6:6: Knowing this, that our old man is crucified with him, that the body of sin might be destroyed, that henceforth we should not serve sin.*

that henceforth we should not serve sin.

7 For he that is dead is freed from sin.

8 Now if we be dead with Christ, we believe that we shall also live with Him:

9 Knowing that Christ being raised from the dead dieth no more; death hath no more dominion over Him.

10 For in that He died, He died unto sin once; but in that He liveth, He liveth unto God.

11 Likewise reckon ye also yourselves to be dead indeed unto sin, but alive unto God through Jesus Christ our Lord.

12 Let not sin therefore reign in your mortal body, that ye should obey it in the lusts thereof.

13 Neither yield ye your members as instruments of unrighteousness unto sin: but yield yourselves unto God, as those that are alive from the dead, and your members as instruments of righteousness unto God.

14 For sin shall not have dominion over you: for ye are not under the law, but under grace.

Verse 1 asks a question: verses 20 and 21 of chapter 5 say that where sin abounded, grace did much more abound, and where sin reigned unto death, grace reigned through righteousness.

Now what shall we say to these things?

In other words, Paul was saying, "Shall we continue sinning so that grace may abound?" since sin got terrible, and when sin got terrible grace was much greater than sin. Since that's the truth...shall we then continue in sin that grace may abound?

No. Paul says, "Shall we continue to live defeated lives so the grace of God will cover for us?" That's the question he's asking. Shall we just continue to fall, confess, fall, confess, fall through our Christian life, over and over again, because God's love and grace is sufficient?

Verse 2: God forbid. How shall we, that are dead to—have died to sin—continue to live in it? Paul is saying: "Look, if that's your experience you'd better check if you died or not." Look at what the Bible says. Don't try to kill yourself; just accept the fact: God says you're dead. That's the faith that overcomes.

The Bible doesn't stop with a theological salvation where, by position I'm saved and forgiven, but conditionally I'm still a slave to sin.

That's not what the Bible is teaching. No. Verses 4 and 5 tell us now that you've been baptized into the body of Jesus Christ, the result is we now walk in the newness of life. A new walk where old things are passed away; behold, all things have become new, in reality. Look again at the question in verse 2. *How shall we, that are dead to sin, live any longer therein?*

Paul is talking about being dead to sin. He doesn't say dead <u>in</u> sin but dead <u>to</u> sin. That because of death, my death, sin no longer has the power to enslave me.

Verse 3: Know ye not—Paul is saying that as many of us as were baptized <u>into</u> Jesus Christ—note the word into again—were baptized into His death?

Paul is not talking about water baptism here. He's saying if you have been conjoined—if you're a Siamese twin with Jesus Christ in His death—that means you died with Him.

If one girl would have died—which she did—so did the other one. Because they had two heads and one body, and it was an amazing thing. I read the whole story. This was the truth. They could write with two heads. They went to Sunday School class, and the two heads worked so closely together that one hand could write what the two heads thought.

I'm bringing this out simply to remind you that's what we are in Christ Jesus. We need to accept that by faith. That is the victory that overcomes the world.

There is no victory in anything less.

Water baptism only signifies the spiritual. Paul is saying that deliverance from sin's power comes because we were baptized spiritually into Christ's death.

> He doesn't say dead in sin but dead to sin.

We were made a Siamese twin with Jesus in His death. We died with Christ.

Verse 4 says: There is a new walk and life based upon a previous death.

Paul says, "Just as Christ resurrected from the dead by the glory of the Father, so the Christian is given the power to resurrect in the newness of life."

That means a life of power over sin.

Now when I was crucified with Christ, the body of sin was destroyed.

That's what the Bible says. He says: "We were crucified with Christ so that the body of sin might be destroyed."

Paul says, "This is the body of sin—where sin grows or is fed." And Paul said it was destroyed at the crucifixion of Christ that we henceforth (from here on) should not serve sin.

I told you that the body of sin is what we inherited from Adam, the natural gravitation to go wrong.

I illustrated it last night with pornography or

whatever—dirty jokes—things you gravitated towards and loved, listened to, and laughed about when you were living in sin. When you got saved, suddenly those things were horrible.

Why was it horrible? Because your new Spirit had taken residence in your heart. The old man was crucified, slain. Now the new man abhorred these things.

A destroying force came and destroyed the old man in you and your natural gravitation. Yes, you may fall. You may sin, but the first thought when you see those sinful things or hear those dirty jokes again is an abhorrence towards it.

Why? Because a new Spirit has taken over. The old body of sin was crucified with Christ. Paul assumes that this is the condition of all believers. He's saying all true believers have died. Verse 7: *For he that is dead is freed from sin.* This is an established fact; this is not something we try to experience, but by faith we accept this as a fact.

One of the greatest mistakes for Christians is to try to make happen what God says has already happened. If you don't take God at His Word for what did happen already, you will try to make it happen.

Verse 8: *Now if we be dead with Christ, we believe that we shall also live with Him.* Verse 9: (Knowing) connects it with verse 8. If we believe we are dead with Christ, we believe that we shall also live with Him, knowing that Christ, being raised from the dead, dieth no more.

I want you to listen carefully to these words.

Christ being raised from the dead, dieth no more; death hath no more dominion over Him. (10) *For in that He died, He died unto sin once: but in that He liveth, He liveth unto God.*

Look at verse 11. *Likewise reckon ye also yourselves to be dead indeed unto sin, but alive unto God through Jesus Christ our Lord.*

Let's take special note of that word reckon. I said last night that reckoning does not create reality.

A lot of people read this and it will say, "Reckon yourself to be dead unto sin." Well, they find that their life has been a failure and so they say, "I must not be dead unto sin, so I'm going to try to kill myself."

I'm not talking about physical death.

Instead of reckoning themselves to be already dead, they go about trying to kill or cripple themselves into submission.

That's not what it means.

It says reckon ye yourselves to be dead. Reckoning is reflecting upon the reality of what already has happened. You don't make things happen by reckoning.

Reckoning is accepting what has already happened. Taking God at His Word.

Let's take note of a word: Likewise. It simply means, "In the same way."

Look again at verses 9 & 10. *Christ being raised from the dead, dieth no more; death hath no more dominion over Him.*

> Instead of reckoning themselves to be already dead, they go about trying to kill or cripple themselves into submission.

No more power over Him.

For in that He died, He died unto sin once: not again and again.

Likewise—in the same way—reckon ye yourself to be dead, once! You died once! You are not going to die again and again, you died once.

Why is this so important? Without accepting this fact, that the old man is dead, we will continue to live defeated lives. If we don't believe he is dead, we will continue to try to put him to death, with numerous applications.

This is nothing less than what the Catholics believe when they do penance, trying to kill the old man or at least bring him into submission. And it goes farther than that.

The Faith That Overcomes

What about the catechism?

What about the certain life that you're supposed to live to curb the flesh? You curb the flesh by faith and that is that! Christ has died and you died with Him.

The flesh loves all kinds of restrictions, as long as it can live in some other areas.

Some of us have been raised with the idea that if you enjoy something it must be wrong. Let's not get carried away with the opposite extreme, and feed the flesh.

God wants us to enjoy life.

We used to think, "What if, at the end of life's road, I have lived this certain life and denied myself this, and I find that I didn't make it anyway. I might as well have fed the flesh."

The old man feeds and grows on self-inflicted punishment.

Monks try to please God in everything they do so they can gain merit with God. The flesh feeds on pulling themselves up by their own bootstraps.

God said, "It's finished." The work is finished and He wants us to accept that, then out of love and gratitude serve Him in humility.

What is the difference between trying to die daily and reckoning myself already dead? The one is trying to make myself acceptable to God, while the other is accepting my position in Christ. The one is trying to gain confidence by experience, while the other will gain experience by confidence. The one is striving to live for Christ, while the other is living by Christ in Him.

In short, the one is trusting; the other is trying.

The faith that overcomes is not a faith to accomplish something, but a faith that accepts what has been accomplished.

Jesus said, "It is finished." The same is true about our resurrection in Christ.

Verse 11 doesn't just say we are to reckon ourselves dead unto sin, but also alive unto God.

It's as important to reckon our self alive unto God as it is dead unto sin. One is as important as the other.

If we don't believe, we'll lack power because we'll lack assurance. And assurance does not come by performance.

I studied for a message I preached one time: "The Conscience and the Bible."

It's amazing. Some people crawl on their hands and knees over rocks for miles to gain confidence in Christ. When they've crawled their tenth mile, their assurance is not any higher!

> *The faith that overcomes is not a faith to accomplish something, but a faith that accepts what has been accomplished.*

But let that person look at God's Word and find that Jesus Christ died for his sins and the conscience will instantly attach itself to that and that person will be set free in a moment.

Why? Because the same hand that wrote the Bible made man's conscience. They both have the same author.

The Christian does not "do" in order to become. He "does" because he is what God has made him in Christ Jesus.

The faith that overcomes is the faith that identifies me with Christ. Where I accept by faith what the Bible teaches regardless what my experience has been in the past.

That by faith I'm as dead as Christ was dead, as alive as Christ was alive, and as righteous as Christ is righteous.

Faith in this Bible truth is what overcomes the world. Anything short of this will stir within us a drive for performance and acceptance.

Now perhaps you have some questions?

What about the cross Jesus tells us to bear? Am

I not daily supposed to pick up my cross and follow Christ? Is that not a commandment from God's Word? If I am dead what's this cross talking about?

For many years I believed the Christian's cross was that which he was to implement into his daily experience. That the old man must daily be crucified in order that the Spirit may have free reign in the believer's life.

But that kind of theory creates a serious problem, and here's the problem.

If the Christian's cross, which Jesus said he is to bear daily, where the old man is to be put to death daily—and the self, then what Paul taught in the epistles contradicts what Jesus taught in the gospel.

Why would Jesus leave behind a gospel that teaches the daily crucifixion of the old man when Paul tells us that the old man was already crucified with Him?

Let's look at II Corinthians 4… Paul talks about being delivered unto death for Jesus' sake. Verse 10: *Always bearing about in the body the dying of the Lord Jesus.*

Now many Christian use these scriptures to teach others of the need to crucify the flesh, dying to self-will and dying to the old man every day. But that is not what Paul is teaching. Look at the context. The whole context is about the physical, not the spiritual.

Verse 7 talks about our bodies—our literal bodies, as earthen vessels.

Verse 9: He's talking about physical persecution.

Verse 10: The physical body again.

Verse 11 talks about being delivered unto physical death—for Jesus' sake.

Verse 16 talks about the outward man perishing, yet the inward man renewed day by day.

It's very clear that the death Paul was talking about is the physical. It is not talking about some self-life or old man, etc. It's clearly the mortal flesh.

I Corinthians 15:30-31: Paul says, "I die daily." What's he talking about?

Again he's talking about physical death, yet many make application here for the spiritual.

Verse 30: The jeopardy that Paul was talking about was to the physical well-being.

Look. Verse 32: Is fighting with wild beasts at an arena physical or spiritual?

We know the answer. Paul was simply saying, "My life is always in jeopardy" when he says, "I die daily." "I'm constantly in danger of losing my life."

He says, "If I have fought with beasts at Ephesus,"

he's talking about physical fighting with beasts in an arena. They turned a wild beast loose to see who would win and gave Paul a sword. Paul fought wild beasts and killed them or he wouldn't have survived. He refers back to that. It was all physical.

What Paul is saying, when he says, "I die daily," is like what David said when he said, "There is but a step between me and death."

If you can find anything in the scripture that I'm missing, I'd like to know it.

Where does this teaching of dying to self-life come from?

I find that this teaching came from the monks. It was handed down to the Catholics and adopted by the Protestants. It's the easy way out. Trying to afflict myself instead of walking by faith. Trying to get rid of the old man that the Bible says is crucified.

Now what about bearing the cross? Jesus taught it. Let's look at these scriptures in Matthew 10:31-39.

31 Fear ye not therefore, ye are of more value than many sparrows. 32 Whosoever therefore shall confess me before men, him will I confess also before my Father which is in heaven. 33 But whosoever shall deny me before men, him will I also deny before my Father which is in heaven. 34 Think not that I am come to send peace on earth: I came not to send peace, but a sword. 35 For I am come to set a man at variance against his father, and the daughter against her mother, and the daughter-in-law against her mother-in-law. 36 And a man's foes shall be they of his own household. 37 He that loveth father or mother more than me is not worthy of me: and he that loveth son or daughter more than me is not worthy of me. 38 And he that taketh not his cross, and followeth after me, is not worthy of

me. 39 He that findeth

Where does this teaching of dying to self-life come from?

his life shall lose it: and he that loseth his life for my sake shall find it.

The context is very clear. Verse 38: *He that taketh not his cross, and followeth after me, is not worthy of me.* Verse 39: *He that findeth his life shall lose it: and he that loseth his life for my sake shall find it.*

Again this talks about physical life. This was before Jesus died, and He is challenging His disciples to follow Him and not to save their life but to offer up their physical life as He offered up His life for the gospel's sake. He's challenging them to be faithful unto the end and not to deny the Lord, like Peter did.

Now, let's remember, in the garden when the

soldiers came to take Jesus, if Peter would have stood up in front and said, "Listen, this is the Son of God. He's done nothing wrong," they would have probably captured Peter and taken him in front of Herod as well. And if Peter had stood in front of the crowd and said, "I testify I have been with this man for three years. This man is the Son of God. He is the power of God come down," there might have been four crosses on the hill. Peter would have taken up his cross and followed Christ. That's what Jesus is talking about here very clearly.

Matthew 16:21-26.

21 *From that time forth began Jesus to show unto His disciples, how that He must go unto Jerusalem, and suffer many things of the elders and chief priests and scribes, and be killed, and be raised again the third day. 22 Then Peter took Him, and began to rebuke Him, saying, Be it far from thee, Lord: this shall not be unto thee. 23 But He turned, and said unto Peter, Get thee behind me, Satan: thou art an offense unto me: for thou savorest not the things that be of God, but those that be of men. 24 Then said Jesus unto His disciples, If any man will come after me, let him deny himself, and take up his cross, and follow me. 25 For whosoever will save his life shall lose it:*

and whosoever will lose his life for my sake shall find it. 26 For what is a man profited, if he shall gain the whole world, and lose his own soul? Or what shall a man give in exchange for his soul?

Mark 8:31-38 deals with Christ's physical sufferings. He challenges His disciples to follow Him and not avoid physical death by denying Him.

Search it out for yourself. Matthew 16:21-26, Mark 8:31-38, also Mark 10:21, Luke 9:24-25, Luke 14:26, and John 19:17-19.

How do we apply these scriptures today? How do we take up the cross and follow Him? If we'd be missionaries and be spreading the gospel in a hostile country and we'd get caught we'd have a choice. We could take up our cross or we could deny it. Let's say armed men would come and lay a Bible up front here and they'd make everybody walk past that Bible and they'd give them a choice.

A man standing beside the Bible with a gun would say, "When you walk past, if you spit on the Bible, you can go out that door. If you don't, I'll shoot you." You'd have a choice: take up your cross, follow Christ, and be shot…or deny Him. Search it out. He's talking about the physical: either saving or losing our lives. He that will save his life shall lose it, and he that will lose his life for my sake shall gain it.

If you start passing out tracts in town and a man bashes you in the face for it, you might have started taking up your cross.

Don't try to implement this cross into trying to kill the old man when he's dead. Accept the fact that you're dead and then you'll have victory.

What about mortifying the deeds of the body? Where does that come in with this thought of the old man or this self being crucified?

Am I not to put to death the deeds of the body? Am I not to bring my body into subjection? Absolutely.

Let's find out how.

Colossians 3:1-10.

1 *If ye then be risen with Christ, seek those things which are above, where Christ sitteth on the right hand of God. 2 Set your affection on things above, not on things on the earth. 3 For ye are dead, and your life is hid with Christ in God. 4 When Christ, who is our life, shall appear, then shall ye also appear with Him in glory. 5 Mortify therefore your members which are upon the earth; fornication, uncleanness, inordinate affection, evil concupiscence, and covetous-*

ness, which is idolatry: 6 For which things' sake the wrath of God cometh on the children of disobedience: 7 In the which ye also walked sometime, when ye lived in them. 8 But now ye also put off all these; anger, wrath, malice, blasphemy, filthy communication out of your mouth. 9 Lie not one to another, seeing that ye have put off the old man with his deeds; 10 And have put on the new man, which is renewed in knowledge after the image of Him that created Him.

Verse 5 says we are to mortify our members. We are to bring them under control. The word mortify means to make noneffective what the flesh wants.

Make it simple.

We all like to eat, many of us more than we should. Is the appetite wrong?

No.

Is eating wrong?

No.

Is overeating wrong?

Yes.

All right. So how do you bring that habit of overeating into submission? How do you mortify that desire to eat more than you should?

Let's read on. Our appetites, fornication, uncleanness, inordinate affections, evil concupiscence, and covetousness, which is idolatry.

Verse 3 tells us how it is done. *Ye are dead. Ye are dead; your life is hid with Christ in God.*

Therefore, because ye are dead and your life is hid with Christ in God, because ye are one with Christ, by claiming this promise, we are to mortify our members.

So you go to church, you have a fellowship meal; you haven't eaten breakfast and you're hungry. You get a big piece of pie and you eat it. You'd like to have another piece. The flesh would say, "I'd like to have it," and you say to the flesh, "I am dead."

"I am dead. I will not." And God, that very instant, will give you power not to. That is reckoning yourself dead—not trying to kill yourself.

We mortify the deeds of the body by believing we are already crucified with Christ. The power to overcome is in accepting the settled facts. Not in trying to accomplish them.

Verse 9: *Lie not one to another.*

Why not? Why not lie one to another?

Seeing ye have put off the old man with his deeds.

Again, very clear. *And have put on the new man, which is renewed in knowledge after the image of Him that created Him.*

Again, it's believing in the established work of the past that gives strength over temptation for the present.

> The only way we can love Him is when we believe we are accepted by Him.

Isaiah 30:15: *In quietness and confidence shall be your strength*. The bottom line is, the only service that is acceptable to God is that which is done out of love for Him.

The only way we can love Him is when we believe we are accepted by Him.

The Bible says, *We love Him, because He first loved us*. Until we believe that we are loved and accepted by God, we will do everything to be accepted and things are done out of duty instead of gratitude.

People can't be whipped into love or brought to a deeper love by condemnation. It might take condemnation to see where they are at. Then they need to go to the cross, and by faith apply what the Word says. And then, out of love, serve the Lord with a free heart. Until then, life is nothing but slavery, in bondage and not free in Christ.

The faith that overcomes is the faith that the old man is…not tries to be…dead, and the new man is Christ Himself, resurrected in me.

Faith in that fact that *I am crucified with Christ,*

nevertheless I live, yet not I, but Christ liveth in me.
Faith in that is the faith that overcomes.

May God be praised.

All right. Let's have that family up here again tonight to sing that song.

Are you ready for it?

> *I am crucified with Christ, nevertheless I live,*
> *Yet not I, but Christ liveth in me,*
> *And the life which I now live in the flesh,*
> *I live by the faith of the Son of God,*
> *Who loved me and He gave Himself for me.*
>
> *Who loved me. Who loved me. Who loved me*
> *And He gave Himself for me.*
> *Who loved me. Who loved me. Who loved me*
> *And He gave Himself for me.*
>
> *If ye then be risen with Christ,*
> *Seek those things which are above,*
> *Where Christ sitteth on the right hand of God.*
> *Set your affections on things above,*
> *Not on things of the earth;*
> *Ye are dead and your life is hid with Christ in God.*
>
> *Ye are dead, Ye are dead, Ye are dead*
> *And your life is hid with Christ in God.*
> *Ye are dead, Ye are dead, Ye are dead*
> *And your life is hid with Christ in God.*

hall we pray?

Father, we come before You this morning, to worship You, to praise You, and thank You, Lord, for the voices that with one accord praised You. I thank You, Father, that You have ordained the church. You've called out of all people, races and tongues, brought together a multitude of people from different cultures and thoughts, Lord, and have named it the church, where Your tell us through Your Word, that You will dwell there.

I thank You, Lord, for the inspiration we can be to one another. The blessing it is to know brothers and sisters in the Lord, that we have this oneness among us, though we have never met before. What a miracle of grace! Father, this morning we also sense a real need for the church to go on, the people of the living God, as we sang, that they would go on and that they would grow in grace, Lord.

Father, I pray that through Your Word You would teach us this morning, the way of grace, of truth, to go on, and to grow. I ask You to be in our midst here through the Holy Ghost, Father, to bless us and to minister to us, that we could go from here with renewed vigor and purpose of heart. With a renewed mind, Father, renewed by the Holy Ghost, through Your Word. I pray, dear God, that Your truth would continue to set us free and we would experience that liberty that is in Jesus Christ only.

I pray, Father, for clarity of thought, and for the ability to put into words the thoughts You give me. Allow this poor vessel, Lord, to be an instrument in Your hand. I pray for sanctified hearts, and for ears that can hear, Lord. I pray that You would hinder every work of darkness, and everything that hinders Your Word from reaching hearts and changing lives. I ask these things in the worthy name of Jesus our Lord. Amen.

"Temptations lose their power when Thou art nigh." I love that phrase in the song we sang. "Temptations lose their power when Thou art nigh."

How and when does the Lord draw nigh? When we draw nigh to Him. James tells us: *Draw nigh unto the Lord and He will draw nigh unto thee.*

How do we draw nigh unto the Lord?

> "Temptations lose their power when Thou art nigh."

By faith. This weekend we've been talking about drawing nigh unto the Lord.

I want to continue on with my message theme: "The Faith That Overcomes," but this morning the title of that theme is "The Faith Defined."

We want to focus on this faith and see where we are at in relating to it.

I read my first scripture in John. *And this is the victory that overcometh the world, even our faith.* Even our faith. Let's take a deep look at this faith.

What are we looking at when we talk about the faith that overcomes? It's not <u>a</u> faith. It's <u>the</u> faith.

Let's define this. We want to annualize the faith once delivered to the saints of old, and find out the nature of this faith. We want to look at the multiple aspects of it and see what it does in the life of one who has it.

There are countless books, articles and sermons preached about the faith. A lot of different theories are in print, and it can get confusing what the faith is. Over the years men have tried to persuade others on their view of the faith. The Bible says there is one faith.

It's the faith, not a faith.

As a boy growing up I used to look at faith as multiple kinds of faith. I never looked at the faith. I looked at a faith. The way I was brought up was one faith. I looked at the Amish faith, the Mennonite faith, the Baptist faith, and I could go on, of the different denominations and churches that profess to be Christian. Yet my life was a culture. I looked at it as the faith.

Look. The faith will produce something in a person's life, but it's far beyond culture. It's the faith, not a faith.

Well, over the years men have tried to persuade others in their view of the faith the Bible speaks about. Consequently the faith once delivered to the saints has been defined as anything from a culture to some kind of a subjected state of mind where you make yourself believe something. For instance, Vincent Peale's book: *Positive Thinking*.

I'll be blunt with you. Once the last book, the last article has been written defining the faith, once the last person has given his view, the Bible will still be the best expository available.

Let's turn our Bibles to Hebrews 11.

Saving faith is in its very nature, saving. Many think of saving faith as only future. Something that will help you in the future as rescuing the soul at death. From final perdition. This is a great and grave mistake. It's a grievous mistake, but many look at it that way.

Christian faith is what orders people's lives. It's what people live by—not only what people will die for—but what they live for daily. They are saved here first, then saved hereafter, because they were first saved here. You don't get saved at death. If faith ever saves the soul, it must first be saved here on earth while the person is making voluntary choices. You know, faith saves souls into happiness in heaven, because it first saved them into holiness on earth. Let's remember that. The faith that overcomes is the faith that saves a person first here on earth into holiness.

If we don't have the faith that keeps us and delivers us from the power of present sins, we do not have the saving faith the Bible talks about. The key to saving faith is to believe without seeing, to believe without experiencing, and to believe without any evidence. That's saving faith, without any tangible evidence.

Let's look at what the Bible says that saving faith

is, the faith delivered to the saints. Hebrews 11: I encourage you to read it often. It's one of my favorite chapters in the Bible.

As a young man 28 years old, with four children, before I was saved, going to church, the first services after communion were always read from Hebrews 11. And the first verse in this chapter was the verse that turned my world upside down. I looked at this verse—Hebrews 11:1 in German:

> *If we don't have the faith that keeps us and delivers us from the power of present sins, we do not have the saving faith the Bible talks about.*

Der Glaube ist ein gewisse Zuversicht des, das man hofft, und ein Nichtzweifeln an dem, das man nicht sieht.

I read that and I reread that, and I read it again, and I knew something was wrong. I dissected this verse, as an unconverted man.

I took it word for word. If the faith that the Bible speaks about is defined here in this verse, then I want to know what it means. I went to the ministers.

My dad was a minister for over forty years and I took that verse to him.

I was taught from childhood up that "der gewisse Glauben ist ein irre Glauben." That means "assurance of salvation is a belief that is unsound."

So, I looked at this. *Der Glaube ist eine gewisse Zuversicht.* I went to the ministers and asked, "What does "Zuversicht" mean?"

My dad said it means "confident." Okay, that sounds pretty good.

What does "gewisse" mean?

<u>And everybody was stuck</u>, because we were told "der gewisse Glauben," (assurance of salvation) is wrong. And gewisse simply means positive confidence. So I asked the ministers, "What does gewisse confidence mean?"

Do you know what it means in German? Gewisse Glauben! And yet I was taught all my life that der gewisse Glauben is of the devil. And here the Bible says, Der Glaube ist eine gewisse confidence!

Well, that verse was the beginning of our search, and it ended up with us getting saved.

The Martin Luther translation is even clearer than King James. Let me translate the German into everyday English. I love the German; in a lot of verses it's almost clearer. The German language has been known to be very expressive. And this is what it says: Now faith is the positive confidence in that which we expect and doesn't even waver in that which we cannot see. Isn't that beautiful?

What have I been talking about this week?

We need the faith. That is the faith that will overcome the world. Positive confidence is something we cannot even see.

We could go into all kinds of commentaries and translations to search out the true meaning of verse one, but there is a better commentary: how it is defined in the lives of the people in the rest of the chapter.

Verse 2 says that by faith—the faith that I just described in verse one—that by this faith the elders obtained a good report.

> *N*ow faith is the positive confidence in that which we expect and doesn't even waver in that which we cannot see.

Verse 3 gives a clue of the true meaning God expects His children to have of the faith. It says that the spoken Word of God is sufficient evidence, sufficient reason for the things that are seen. We don't need any explanation. The fact that the morning dawns and the sun comes up—that's sufficient evidence that there's a God. Because God's Word says so. That's all we need. We don't need some scientific evidence; we don't need some proof.

It's amazing. God never tries to prove His existence. The Bible says: *In the beginning, God...* That's all. I want you to understand one thing: the spoken Word of God is all we need for sufficient evidence to trust Him. That's all we need.

We don't need any new revelation. Creation, which our eyes behold, was brought about by that which is not even seen. In other words, we are to believe God's Word, regardless of evidence or experience.

> In other words, we are to believe God's Word, regardless of evidence or experience.

Believing means to act upon that which has no tangible evidence to support it. I want you to take note of verse 6. Without such a faith that I've described, it's not possible to please God. For he that comes to God, draws nigh to God and wants God to draw nigh to him.

We said we draw nigh to God by faith, and when we draw nigh to God, He will draw nigh to us. What happens when God draws nigh to us? "<u>Temptations lose their power</u> when Thou art nigh." God wants us to draw nigh to Him—it's not possible to please Him until we do, for we must believe that the Unseen exists, and that He will reward those who diligently seek Him.

The faith that pleases God also believes in God's goodness. It believes in God's loving-kindness and tender mercies, that God rewards the seeker, blesses him, and draws nigh to him. That's the faith that overcomes.

Verse 13 says, *These all died in faith, not having received the promises, but having seen them afar off, and were persuaded of them, and embraced them, and confessed that they were strangers and pilgrims on the earth.* These all died, not having received what their faith told them existed, with no tangible evidence. But look what their faith accounted to! They were persuaded and embraced what they had no tangible evidence of. And then what happened? They confessed that they were strangers and pilgrims on earth.

Beloved, this is not written to give us facts on history. Yes, it does that, but it's much more. This is to give us a very clear definition of the faith that overcomes, to give direction how we are to relate to God's promises.

Relating to our salvation, to our justification, to our sanctification; that's what this is written for.

You'll find when you read the Old Testament, what God promised to them was basically physical and tangible. What God promises us in these exceedingly great and precious promises in His Word, that makes us partakers of the divine nature, is spiritual. It's spiritual; it's no longer tangible.

God wants us to relate to these spiritual promises like they related to their tangible or their physical ones.

We are to believe without seeing. We are to embrace what we cannot see. We are to accept God's promises in His Word even though we have no tangible evidence that it's there or that it's working, or that I'm experiencing it, or that I'm feeling it. We are to embrace it just the same.

After all, God measures our spiritual progress by our faith, not by our experience.

Once we accept our justification and our sanctification that way, we too will become strangers and pilgrims on this earth. This is the faith that overcomes.

People read God's Word, they'll see a promise in God's Word, and they think they have this faith apart from His Word, and they'll bring it to the Word and apply it to the Word.

It's nothing but a subjective state of mind to where they think they have now conquered, and now they want to bring this subjective state of mind, and release that upon some promise that God makes.

That's not saving faith.

Listen, faith is not some kind of resource that you and I go to or have that you can release to make your life better in trouble and difficulties.

No, that's not Bible-believing faith. The faith that we talk about is not a resource that we are to perform some self-indulging miracles with.

When the Word says, have faith in God, immediately many read it like this: <u>have faith</u> in God instead of have <u>faith</u> in <u>God</u>.

You see the object. Today more focus is on faith instead of God.

But faith is not to be the focus; it's to be the object of faith that needs to be the focus. God needs to be the focus, not faith. The Bible says Jesus Christ is the author and finisher of our faith. The focus needs to be Jesus Christ.

Many try to create the faith first, and then bring it to God. They try to feel and stir up the faith by their emotions before they will commit themselves.

Let me give you an illustration of this. If I would walk up to you and ask, "Are you saved?"

You know the first thing that happens? The first thing that tends to happen is we try to feel saved. Before we give an answer we want to feel saved.

Let me give you a key to victory. God created us so that you cannot feel faith by trying to feel. The mind needs an object to focus upon before it can feel.

Now, if I'd ask, "What think ye of Christ?"

Immediately your mind would have an object to focus on.

Then I would say some words such as whipping post. Spikes. Weeping mother. Spit, slaps, crown of thorns.

All of these are putting something in your mind that you're focusing on and you're finishing what I mentioned a portion of. Then I could ask you the question again: "What think ye of Christ?"

> Today more focus is on faith instead of God.

Emotions and feelings surface, because your mind has an object of focus. Out of that comes feeling. What think ye of Christ is going to determine whether or not you are saved. Not whether you have some kind of feeling.

Put it this way. If I would take one of these bright lights and put my hand in front, it would make a shadow like my body is now making a shadow here.

Now if I step away from the light, there will be no shadow regardless how bright the light is. That light has to have an object before it will create a shadow.

The shadow is your feelings. The object is what your mind is focused on.

You don't create feelings by trying to feel. You've

> *What think ye of Christ is going to determine whether or not you are saved. Not whether you have some kind of feeling.*

got to have an object of focus. So when I ask you, "Are you saved?" the first thing that happens is you try to feel saved.

No. If I ask you, "Are you saved?" you need to think: What does the Word say? Who is Christ? What did He do for me?

The Word says that if I believe in Him I am saved. I can with confidence say, "I believe in Him." I don't have to look for feelings; they will come later.

Don't be led through your life by feelings. There are a lot of people today that are so introspective they can't enjoy their Christian lives. One day they feel like they're saved. The next, they don't have that assurance; they don't feel saved today, so they think they're not saved.

Look! Your Christian life is not lived in your emotions. Your Christian life is lived in your will. You will to serve God, and when you will to serve God, forget your feelings. They'll follow after if you let them, but if you're going to bring them to the surface all the time and try to judge your life by your feelings, you're going to have ups and downs all the time.

Go by the Word. It will not fail. Long after your

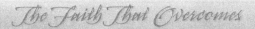

feelings and emotions are dirt and you're buried six feet under, the Word will say what it says.

Feelings are not to be the focus. Faith is not to be the focus. Some try to speak the faith and come to God and present it to Him.

This is very popular among some groups today—the "name it and claim it" gospel. They speak their faith. Then they expect God to respond to that self-manufactured positive thinking. That's all it is.

I remember a woman my wife and I knew quite well. She got sidetracked into this positive thinking; this "name it and claim it" gospel. And I know what they say. I've read books about it.

I know one instance where a man was a multi-millionaire, and yet he wanted another big tract of land. He looked at his bank account and knew he didn't have the money to buy it, but he went and looked at the land and said to God, "I'm going to have it. That is mine."

And he expected that faith in the words spoken would create something to bring about his purchase of it.

And believe me, some of that stuff works. God gave them their request but sent leanness to their soul. We'd better be careful about these things.

But I remember this woman; she was under some of this teaching, and her child ran and opened the screen door. The spring slipped off and the end of the spring flew into his eye, blinding him. She took him to the doctor, and he was blind.

This woman wrote us a letter, and this is what she wrote—I forgot the little boy's name, but I'll call him Johnny—she said, "Little Johnny is blind, but he can see." Do you know what she was doing? She was convincing herself that Johnny can see, and she figured that if she convinced herself, she will bring this self-convincing attitude to God and God will make him see.

That's not faith; that's positive thinking.

That's no better than Vincent Peale and his book of positive thinking.

The faith that overcomes is not separate from God; it's not some subjected state of mind that we bring to God for Him to honor. In other words, when you look at God's promises like this, you read God's Word and find a promise. You don't hold off from applying God's promises until you have manu-factured enough faith to apply it or until you have enough positive thoughts that you can apply it.

No, you look at God's Word, and as you read

God's Word you accept it for what it is—truth that can not lie. You don't try to hold off from applying it to your life. You apply it whether you feel like it or not!

You just step out and commit yourself to this promise. You don't wait until you've manufactured some faith so you feel better about applying it.

> *Y*ou don't hold off from applying God's promises until you have manufactured enough faith to apply it...

We must remember that faith comes by hearing, and hearing by the Word of God. That's what the Bible tells us in Romans 10:17. In other words it's the hearing or the reading of the Word that creates faith.

You don't create faith and then bring it to some promise. No. That's not the way it works.

It's the promise itself that creates that faith in you to commit yourself to it.

Remember what Peter says about this in II Peter 1:4. *Whereby are given unto us exceeding great and precious promises, that by these promises ye are made partakers of the divine nature.* By these promises.

Let me illustrate this. In verse 13 of our text it says, These all died in faith. That means they all died in the state of faith. It says nothing of their feelings. It says nothing of their doubts or anything.

I want this message to anchor you in the faith once delivered to the saints to where it will change your life. I want that to happen. That's my prayer this morning. Because it can change your way of thinking. It can change your life.

But let's look at this. When it says these all died in faith, that means they all died in the state of faith. Not having received the promises, but having seen them afar off. They only read of them or heard of them—however God communed with them; they saw them afar off. They saw the invisible. Their response to seeing God's promise was that they were persuaded of them.

Just this morning we sang these words: "And faith taking hold of the Word," and what happened... "My fetters fell off, and I anchored my soul."

Faith taking hold of the Word. They were persuaded. God's promises themselves produced a persuasion in the people in chapter 11.

"And these exceeding great and precious promises are what brought the divine nature." What is the divine nature? It's the power of God...the Holy Spirit within a person.

But what happened was God spoke. God promised and the promise itself created faith in them.

They were persuaded and embraced these promises. Whenever someone is persuaded of a promise…the natural response is to embrace it. Until you embrace it you're not persuaded.

If you cannot embrace the fact that the Bible tells you that you can believe that you're saved, then you're not persuaded of the trustworthiness of it. Once you're persuaded of a promise in God's Word you will naturally respond and embrace it.

You'll make it part of your commitment and make it part of your life.

That's Bible-believing faith.

The faith that overcomes is following God regardless. Regardless is what makes it faith.

Now let's look at another aspect of this faith. The faith that is tried in verse 17. *By faith Abraham, when he was tried, offered up Isaac.*

This word tried is a very important word when it comes to the faith that overcomes. Faith reaches its highest quality, its highest potential, <u>only when tried</u>. The problem is we are too carnal minded to see that way.

But remember. Faith that is not tried is not a deep and abiding faith. That's why God brings trials into our lives.

He wants us to have a deep and abiding faith. If the faith that overcomes is to live out its fullest potential, it's got to have an alternative.

The alternative is doubt. You have to be able to doubt before faith can have its highest potential.

The same way, love has no meaning if you cannot hate. It loses all its meaning.

The free will means nothing if you cannot choose to do the opposite.

That's what Christian virtue is all about. Christian virtue loses all its meaning if you cannot choose to do what you shouldn't do. But to make a right choice when you could make a wrong choice; that's Christian virtue.

The tree of life had to have an alternative. It's amazing. There are people going around saying, "We don't have a will."

Let me tell you a secret. If you don't have a will, you can't be tempted.

You can't.

The fact that you have a will and you can choose against what God wants is what makes temptation possible. The devil comes and tempts you with something and the strength

> If you cannot embrace the fact that the Bible tells you that you can believe that you're saved then you're not persuaded of the trustworthiness of it.

in the temptation is: you can decide, I will go along with what the devil suggests, or I will not.

You have the power. When God gave man a free will He gave him a power of his own. If Eve could not have chosen

But to make a right choice when you could make a wrong choice; that's Christian virtue.

to eat the forbidden fruit, she could not have been tempted by the devil and he wouldn't have wasted his time.

Faith cannot grow without an alternative. Maybe your next trial, this will help you along, because without the trying of our faith, we cannot grow.

Throughout the Old Testament, God gives a promise to each person, and this promise creates faith in the individual.

Like Abraham. He came to Abraham and promised him a son, and that promise inspired Abraham to believe that he would have a son.

What did God do? You'll find it in the Bible over and over again; that instead of immediately receiving that promise (verse 13) the rest of these people's lives is one of trial.

Let me tell you, when you become a Christian and serve the Lord Jesus Christ, the rest of your life is a trial. God allows that trial to perfect your faith.

Why did the children of Israel have so many trials going through the wilderness?

God was preparing them, and every time they failed He said, "Take another lap around the mountain." And this trial that we face is usually directly related to the promise, and the faith that we have concerning that very promise.

ook at these people's lives. God has given them this wonderful promise, and then the rest of their life He's challenging them to see if they lose faith in that promise.

We would think—why doesn't God promise us something and then make sure we're never tempted to doubt that promise?

Our faith would get weaker and weaker. We'd get anemic. No, when God has all His saints gathered around His throne, He wants people that are there of free choice when they could have chosen the opposite.

How pleasant would it be this morning, you husbands, if you knew that your wife was forced to marry you? I can always remember that my wife chose on her own accord and will to marry me or not, and that's a comfort to me.

But you know what? God tries our faith; it's right in between the promise and the fulfillment of that promise that we face these trials.

> Every time your faith is tried and you come out on top of it you are a stronger person in faith.

We're tried, but it's the trying of faith that is precious to God, and causes individuals to bring forth a good report. Verse 7: And to be heir of the righteousness which is by faith. You see the good report is that they hung on when they could have let go, and you and I have that same thing.

Will it be said of us someday—will there be a good report? Because you went through your trials and hung on to what the Word says regardless of your feelings, regardless what evidence you had—you hung on to the Word—you won't get upset or nothing. That's not what it's talking about; it's talking about endurance.

Every time your faith is tried and you come out on top of it you are a stronger person in faith. When the next trial comes along and you remember that other time you were victorious, then that will give you strength to be victorious again. So the trying of your faith worketh endurance.

The patience in the Bible is meant to be endurance. Hanging in there.

I Peter 1:7: *The trial of your faith, being much more precious than of gold that perisheth, though it be tried with fire, might be found unto praise and honor and glory at the appearing of Jesus Christ.*

Hallelujah! The trial of faith. I Peter 4:12: *Beloved, think it not strange concerning the fiery trial which is to try you, as though some strange thing happened unto you.*

God purifies our faith by the trials that we face. Look how God tested Abraham.

Abraham stood on the promise like I told you the other evening—he could have been sitting down at the local country store, when the men were gathered around, talking about their "nochcomashaft"—all their children. They could've been talking about the blessings of being a grandfather, and Abraham is sitting there childless and he smiles at them and says, "I have a million children."

They say, "What's wrong with that guy? He doesn't even have a child, let alone a million. What's the matter with you, Abraham?"

He says, "I have a million children. Hallelujah!"

"You don't have a child!"

Abraham says, "God says I have, and I have, whether I see them or not."

That's how we've got to take God's Word, and let me tell you that is the faith that overcomes. Whether we see it or not. Taking God at His Word.

Abraham sat there waiting and waiting and even got impatient and decided, "I'm going to have to move God along in this thing." So he marries Hagar. It turned out a disaster. Today we have all this fighting in the Middle East because of it.

After Abraham finally received evidence of the promise God had given him, he's got little baby Isaac in his hands. That's evidence of the promise.

And God says, "Abraham, I want you to wipe out all the evidence." Did Abraham have faith?

"I want you to wipe out all visible evidence of the promise; to get rid of the very foundation of your million children, Abraham. Get rid of it."

What was God doing? He was giving Abraham the opportunity to doubt. He was trying Abraham, so that his faith would grow and get stronger.

He was trying to see if Abraham would stand on the promises and believe God even when he had no visible evidence anymore.

Let me tell you, we still have that same God, who longs to see us take Him at His Word with the only evidence: His Word.

The faith that overcomes also delivers from the fear of man.

Look at Hebrews 11:23: *By faith Moses, when he was born, was hid three months by his parents, because they saw he was a proper child; and they were not afraid of the king's commandment.*

By faith Moses' parents disobeyed the government at the risk of being found out, with the death penalty. They just believed God. They took their child, put him in a basket, and committed him to the Lord.

How many of you mothers would want to take a little child, put him in a little basket floating among the bulrushes, and walk away from him?

They trusted God. They cast their bread upon many waters, and their little bread returned unto them, as a potential Pharaoh of the future. One who would deliver God's people.

> Let me tell you, we still have that same God, who longs to see us take Him at His Word with the only evidence: His Word.

The faith that overcomes is also a sanctifying faith. It gives discernment to make right choices:

Hebrews 11:25. Properly calculates the worth and endurance of given situations (Verse 26). Verse 27 is very clear: the faith that overcomes gives grace that endures because it sees beyond the visible.

> *Again faith is that which takes God at His Word regardless whether it makes sense or not.*

Do you see that? It counts those things which be not as though they were.

He believed that which he did not see and the result was it sanctified him. Do you want to be sanctified? Believe without visible evidence. That's what sanctification is all about. Don't let anyone convince you otherwise.

Sanctification is by faith.

It says it sanctified him. He gave up the riches and power of Egypt for the reproach of Christ. Verse 28: He kept the Passover and sprinkling of blood lest He that destroyed the firstborn should touch them.

Again faith is that which takes God at His Word regardless whether it makes sense or not. How much sense did the smearing of the blood on the doorpost make to the children of Israel? How much sense did that make to them on the other side of the cross?

I can well imagine. "That's senseless. That's ridiculous. Why smear blood on the doorpost of the house?"

It didn't make sense. It didn't have to make sense.

Those that did it, did it because they believed what God said, making sense or not.

Moses said, "This is what God is saying; you'd better do it." And they did it.

As we look at the verses in this chapter these people all looked like mighty men of God. You know, giants of faith.

What we read about here in these pages makes us today look so small. It makes us look like we have no faith at all.

But look at this in reality. If you read chapter 11 of Hebrews, all these saints looked like <u>mighty giants</u> of faith, but go back in the Old Testament and read their account, and find out what kind of giants they really were.

Were these people without fault and didn't stumble or fall? Think of all the failures of Abraham. How many times he doubted and stumbled along; yet he is called the father of faith.

How he tried to produce his own miracle with Hagar? That was strictly the outcome of unbelief. He doubted it. That's why he couldn't wait on God; he thought he had to hurry up God on this thing, and it didn't work out.

Think of the four generations of people who lied

to save their skin, because of the poor example of Abraham.

He said, "my wife is my sister." His son repeated the same thing. What happened after that? Isaac's wife lied to Isaac concerning the boys. Jacob lied to his father.

What happened to Jacob's sons? They lied about the whereabouts of Joseph.

You could go on and on, lie after lie, generation after generation. It all started with Abraham.

When you go back to where the children of Israel left Egypt and were up against the Red Sea, and all of a sudden a dust comes up and they look—and behold! Pharaoh's army!

The Red Sea on one side and Pharaoh's army on the other. We call it between a rock and a hard place. And what did they do?

They murmured and cried and were ready to stone Moses. Does it say that in the New Testament?

No, no! Look what it says: Verse 29 says: By faith. By faith?

I mean, they were murmuring.

It says by faith they passed through the Red Sea. It says nothing of their doubt and accusation against Moses.

God looks at the overall view and He says they did it by faith. Isn't God good, loving, and kind. Isn't God gracious?

Do you know what the difference is? The Old Testament is the time of justice and judgment. The New Testament is grace.

You know, it's such a comfort to me. I have so many failures in my life. But you know, it's when a person keeps going, like Abraham. He had failures, he had doubts, but he kept going on. At the end of his life all those failures he made were totally wiped out in Hebrews 11. You will not find one mistake recorded in Hebrews 11 of any of these saints of old.

When we look at Hebrews 11 we can say: "These men were <u>mighty men of God</u>!"

But when you look at their account, they murmured and complained, but they kept going. And the overview of it all was: they died in faith, leaving a good report! Isn't it wonderful?

I'm so glad that God looks at the overview of our lives and doesn't focus on the times of doubt that we go through. He knows our frame. He remembers that we are but dust.

> It says by faith they passed through the Red Sea. It says nothing of their doubt and accusation against Moses.

You know, some of those times of fear, frustration, and complaints, He overrules with an overall work of grace. And He looks at whole the thing as an overall walk of faith, because they continued faithful.

> The Bible says the just man falls seven times but rises again.

It's when we keep going on that God is pleased and counts our life as a life of faith. And that brings about a good report. Our walk is not all a mountaintop experience; there are times we hit a low and stumble and fall. The Bible says the just man falls seven times but rises again.

God tells us to get up and win the race.

Sometimes you read books about some great Christian's walk of faith and you wonder if you even have any faith at all. But these books are just like Hebrews 11—they point out all the high points in a person's life, never mentioning the low, but they were people just like us today.

James reminds us of this concerning Elijah, a man subject to like passions as we are. You know James didn't say anything about the time Elijah said, "Take my life now. I'm the only one left."

God had to remind him that 7,000 did not bow to Baal. But James doesn't mention that doubt. James doesn't mention one time that Elijah ran. He just says he was subject to like passions as we are.

I remember my surprise when I discovered that John Bunyan, a spiritual giant who wrote *Pilgrim's Progress*, struggled with doubts and depression. He had an awful time overcoming that.

Think of the harlot Rahab in verse 31 of our text. Did she have any doubts? Get a picture of what it means to go by the spoken word. How much did she know about the God of Israel? She was a pagan and a harlot.

I can imagine someone questioning Rahab, "Rahab, how was it? How strong was your faith, Rahab?"

I can imagine her saying, "What faith? They just told me to hang out a scarlet cord; they didn't say anything about faith. And I just did it."

That's what I'm talking about. Just do it! Take it for what it says! You'll be rewarded. You'll be saved just like Rahab. Today she's among those who obtained a good report.

You see, God looks at our commitments. He's not so concerned about our fleeting doubts, but our overall commitments.

If you're wondering this morning whether you are saved or not, look at your commitment. Suppose, right here in this setting, you were brought up to the decision, "I'm going to have to either commit myself to what the Word says and go with these people that are walking by faith, or I'm going to go back to the old setting and just let it go. I can't take it.

"The persecution I'm getting. The loss of my family. The loss of my material goods. I can't take it. I'm going back to the old setting."

Well, if that's your case, then God have mercy on you.

But if you're willing to commit yourself, regardless what you lost, but you don't feel very saved…look. God looks at your commitment.

You made your decision that you're going to trust the Word and believe Jesus and it brought about the persecution and the spoiling of your goods. To stand brought about the loss. Listen! Your commitment is what God sees.

If you continue to believe what God's Word says regardless what comes, you'll be of those who are of good report.

God looks at our commitment. I believe we could, profitably, look at each of these remaining verses of this chapter and make application, but for the sake of time we'll move on.

I want to look at the practical aspects and applications of the faith that overcomes that we're talking about. Faith is not some-thing you bring with you in your relationship with God

> *F*aith does not exist apart from the presence and the promises of God.

and then you release it upon some promise.

No. Faith does not exist apart from the presence and the promises of God. Bible faith is not some positive frame of mind that maintains a high morale.

Faith may tremble. Faith may be lowly in demeanor and at times may appear quite weak.

But one thing sure. Divine faith continues going on whether you feel like it or not, whether you have emotions or not. Divine faith will hang on to God's promises regardless of the circumstances.

Faith is an important part of everyone's life! Psychologists say faith is essential to man's physical and mental well-being. People without faith are people of despair and despondency.

There's a deep mystery found in the way man was created, having to do with faith. It's found in every religion, in every culture, or cult. It's found everywhere, this longing within man, this tendency to believe in something.

It's expressed in the way people live and relate to life. It's in every cult or culture. You can go to the remotest parts of the jungle and find a tribe of people that believe in the unseen, something they can't see with tangible evidence.

Man was born that way. Man is not content to believe only in the tangible and the visible. He will continually venture into the realm that can only be experienced by faith. That's why it's so important that man finds the truth, and directs this desire and impulse in the right direction.

I would like to apply the rest of the message to everyday life. The saints in Hebrews 11 were in the old dispensation, where the salvation God would provide was in the future. Today we live in this dispensation on this side of the crucifixion.

We, like them, are called to walk by faith. We are justified by faith just like Abraham was (Romans 4:24).

People without faith are people of despair and despondency.

Now the whole walk of faith primarily has to do with our justification and our sanctification. We need to remember that when Paul wrote Romans chapter 1 through 5 he was preparing them for chapters 6,7 and 8. When he explains in chapters 3,4 and 5 what justification means and how we are justified by faith only, he was preparing us for sanctification in the same way. By faith only.

> It's not what you do for God that sanctifies you; neither is what God does through you what sanctifies you.

The faith that justifies is also the faith that sanctifies. Faith in the death of Christ justifies. And faith in my identity with that death, burial, and resurrection also sanctifies. Colossians 2:6 makes this clear. *As ye have therefore received Christ Jesus so walk ye in Him.* Just like you received Him, that's how you're supposed to walk in Him.

As you have begun your Christian walk so continue to walk. As you were justified so are you sanctified by faith.

It's not what you do for God that sanctifies you. Get that straight.

Most true Christians don't have a hard time accepting that, but listen to this: neither is what God does through you what sanctifies you.

It's not what is happening here and now. It's not what God can do in you now that sanctifies you. No, it's what He has already done for you and to you, 2,000 years ago. Faith in that is what sanctifies you.

Just as we look back 2,000 years ago to Christ's death for our justification so we must look back 2,000 years to our death with Him for our sanctification.

We are to walk by faith in that which is past and not try to re-create our death experience again.

We are dead. We are buried and resurrected with Christ by faith. It's a spiritual death, burial, and resurrection done by God through the Spirit. I Cor. 12:13 calls it a baptism, Col. 2:12 calls it an operation of God.

It says this way: *Buried with Him in baptism, wherein also ye are risen with Him through the faith of the operation of God, who hath raised Him from the dead.*

Romans 6:11 says we are to reckon ourselves to be dead indeed unto sin and alive unto God. I'd like to bring this to your attention: the word "indeed" isn't in there to take up space. It means "for sure." To reckon yourselves dead "for sure."

Let's remember, reckoning does not create reality. Reckoning reflects upon the reality of what God has already spoken.

In other words you don't make things happen by reckoning. Reckoning is accepting what has already happened and taking God at His Word.

We are not sanctified by praying three hours a day. No. Accepting your sanctification by faith may produce three hours of praying a day. Reading ten chapters of God's Word each day will not sanctify you. We are sanctified by taking God at His Word. Now you might read ten chapters a day out of joy of being sanctified. Out of joy of the salvation you experience.

When Jesus said in John 17, "*Sanctify them through thy truth; thy Word is truth,*" He was not saying we are sanctified by how much we read, but by how much we believe what we read. That's how we're sanctified.

The bottom line is this: the faith that overcomes the world is the faith that takes God's Word at face value.

It believes that whatsoever God has promised that He is also able to perform.

The soul that has this faith reflects upon the exceeding great and precious promises of God, and the life within these promises will impart to him the divine nature and he will escape the corruption that is in the world today through lust.

The question may come up: Is it possible for the true Christian to sin?

There are a lot of groups out there that say it is not possible, that if you sin you have never been born again. I disagree. I DIS-AGREE.

> We are sanctified by taking God at His Word.

I'm not a Calvinist. I want that clearly understood.

The question is: Is it possible for the true Christian to sin?

Let me tell you something. As long as we are in this body, it's possible.

But John says: _These things write I unto you, that ye sin not._ _And if any man sin, we have an advocate with the Father, Jesus Christ the righteous._

The Psalmist said it this way. _Thy word have I hid in my heart_—not stored in my head—_thy word have I hid in my heart, that I might not sin against thee._

Now faith is the substance of things hoped for, the evidence of things not seen. Do you and I have that faith that overcomes, and will it be said of us someday that by faith we have obtained a good report?

We're going to have that family come up and sing that song again.

I just want to reinforce every message with that song, because it's so vital.

The song is on page 49.

Father, we have gathered with expectation and, Lord, as we expect You to bless us and as we yield ourselves to You, we will not be disappointed.

Thank You, Father, again for hungry souls. Thank You, Father, for those who truly want to know the truth, to be set free. Thank You, Lord, for the inspiration they can be.

I pray, Lord, that You would visit us again this afternoon at this final meeting.

Lord, open up the windows and give us such a blessing that we cannot contain it, but that it would flow out into other people's lives as well.

Oh, Father, I pray in Jesus' name, set this community on fire. I pray, dear God, that Your Spirit would go up and down these streets in homes and in places, and open up the darkness, Lord. Shine the lights of heaven into the hearts of those buried in religion and darkness, Lord. Oh, Father, reveal Yourself.

I pray that this afternoon would inspire and move us, Lord, to be vessels and channels through which You can flow. That Your name would go forth and be lifted up and receive glory and honor, Lord. You would receive the reward of the suffering that You endured for all of us. Bless us this afternoon, Father. Keep us awake and alert, Lord, by Your Holy Spirit, I pray this in Jesus' name. Amen.

At the final meeting that we have I'd like to thank each one for your attendance and your hunger. It means so much to me.

It inspires me to go on. There are no people easier to preach to than those who are hungry. If a mother spends a lot of time cooking and sets the food on the table and the family gathers around and they fall asleep, there's no hunger there. It's discouraging.

But when the children gather around the table saying, "I'm hungry," it's a wonderful time.

Let's turn our Bible to Matthew 27. The title of my message this afternoon is the mending of the veil. The mending, not the rending. The mending of the veil.

Matthew 27:45-53, verse 45: *Now from the sixth hour there was darkness over all the land unto the ninth hour. 46 And about the ninth hour Jesus cried with a loud voice, saying, Eli, Eli, lama sabachthani? that is to say, My God, my God, why hast thou forsaken me? 47 Some of them that stood there, when they heard that, said, This man calleth for Elijah. 48 And straightway one of them ran, and took a sponge, and filled it with vinegar, and put it on a reed, and gave Him to drink. 49 The rest said, Let be, let us see whether Elijah will come to save Him. 50 Jesus, when He had cried again with a loud voice, yielded up the ghost. 51 And, behold, the veil of the temple was rent in twain from the top to the bottom; and the earth did quake, and the rocks rent; 52 And the graves were opened; and many bodies of the saints which slept arose, 53 And came out of the graves after His resurrection, and went into the holy city, and appeared unto many.*

Mark 15:24-38, verse 24: *And when they had crucified Him, they parted His garments, casting lots upon them, what every man should take. 25 And it was the third hour, and they crucified Him. 26 And the superscription of His accusation was written over, THE KING OF THE JEWS.*

27 And with Him they crucify two thieves; the

one on His right hand, and the other on His left. 28 And the scripture was fulfilled, which saith, And He was numbered with the transgressors. 29 And they that passed by railed on Him, wagging their heads, and saying, Ah, thou that destroyest the temple, and buildest it in three days, 30 Save thyself, and come down from the cross. 31 Likewise also the chief priests mocking said among themselves with the scribes, He saved others; Himself He cannot save. 32 Let Christ the King of Israel descend now from the cross, that we may see and believe. And they that were crucified with Him reviled Him. 33 And when the sixth hour was come, there was darkness over the whole land until the ninth hour. 34 And at the ninth hour Jesus cried with a loud voice, saying, Eloi, Eloi, lama sabachthani? which is, being interpreted, My God, my God, why hast thou forsaken me? 35 And some of them that stood by, when they heard it, said, Behold, He calleth Elijah. 36 And one ran and filled a sponge full of vinegar, and put it on a reed, and gave Him to drink, saying, Let alone; let us see whether Elijah will come to take Him down. 37 And Jesus cried with a loud voice, and gave up the ghost. 38 And the veil of the temple was rent in twain from the top to the bottom.

The Faith That Overcomes

John 19:17-30: Verse 17 *And He bearing His cross went forth into a place called the place of a skull, which is called in the Hebrew Golgotha:* 18 *Where they crucified Him and two others with Him, on either side one, and Jesus in the midst.* 19 *And Pilate wrote a title, and put it on the cross. And the writing was, JESUS OF NAZARETH THE KING OF THE JEWS.* 20 *This title then read many of the Jews: for the place where Jesus was crucified was nigh to the city: and it was written in Hebrew, and Greek, and Latin.* 21 *Then said the chief priests of the Jews to Pilate, Write not, The King of the Jews; but that He said, I am King of the Jews.* 22 *Pilate answered, What I have written I have written.* 23 *Then the soldiers, when they had crucified Jesus, took His garments, and made four parts, to every soldier a part; and also His coat: now the coat was without seam, woven from the top throughout.* 24 *They said therefore among themselves, Let us not rend it, but cast lots for it, whose it shall be: that the scripture might be fulfilled, which saith, They parted my raiment among them, and for my vesture they did cast lots. These things therefore the soldiers did.* 25 *Now there stood by the cross of Jesus His mother, and His mother's sister, Mary the wife of Cleophas, and Mary Magdalene.* 26 *When Jesus therefore saw His mother, and the disciple standing by, whom He loved, He saith unto His mother, Woman, behold thy son! 27 Then saith he to the disciple, Behold thy mother! And from that hour that disciple took her unto his own home. 28 After this, Jesus knowing that all things were now accomplished, that the scripture might be fulfilled, saith, I thirst. 29 Now there was set a vessel full of vinegar: and they filled a sponge with vinegar, and put it upon hyssop, and put it to His mouth. 30 When Jesus therefore had received the vinegar, He said, It is finished: and He bowed His head, and gave up the ghost.*

Now both in Matthew and Mark it tells us that after Jesus gave up the ghost the veil in the temple rent in two from the top to the bottom.

In our text in John 19 it tells us right before Jesus gave up the ghost He said these three words: *It is finished! Es ist vollbracht!*

Before this, verse 28 says Jesus knew all things were now accomplished. Let's remember these words. It was all over. All that Jesus had been sent to accomplish was done. Nothing was left undone. His earthly life was drawing to a close like two mighty curtains in a play being drawn together. Jesus, just before the scene was closed, spoke one last time these words: "It is finished."

These three words were a seal upon His finished work and upon His life of thirty-three years. A period at the end of the sentence of His life. No question mark. No comma. But a solid period. There's nothing to add.

And immediately the curtain in the temple tore from the top to the bottom. It swung wide open in two pieces.

Now according to history, there was activity at the temple at this very moment. The daily sacrificial lamb was being slain and the high priest was going about his daily routine.

I believe he was more than a bit troubled. Some unexplainable things were happening in Jerusalem in the last 24 hours, and it shook the people up.

I believe the high priest, going about sacrificing this lamb, had some deep thoughts. And I believe he was quite shook up. Mark 15:33 tells us that for three hours there was darkness over the whole land.

The people were tense. They didn't know what to make of it. I believe a lot of them had guilty consciences.

You know what happens when you have a guilty conscience. Suddenly it seems like the powers of heaven are taking over. Fear grips the heart.

The high priest, perhaps nervous as he went about

taking care of this sacrifice, went into the Holiest of Holies with the blood of the lamb.

He, alone, was the only person allowed in there, and he was very careful, because if anyone else went in, God struck them dead.

I believe every time the high priest went in, he remembered that he might not come out. Carefully he carried out the orders that God had given them.

You can imagine after there was darkness over the whole earth, perhaps he was smote by his conscience because the Pharisees knew in their hearts that Jesus was a man sent from God.

Nicodemus reveals that much. Nicodemus was of the Sanhedrin, a member of 70 men. And he came to Jesus by night and he says, *"We know…"*

Who is we? The Sanhedrin knew.

"We know that Thou art a teacher sent from God." I believe that this man as he went into the Holiest of Holies with the blood of the lamb was more than a little bit nervous, when suddenly he hears behind him the noise of heavy tearing. He whirls around and is horrified at what took place.

This place that was just for the high priest; this place that no one was allowed to set foot into; this place was suddenly wide open for daylight to stream into and everyone could see what he was doing. The veil rent and the whole place was wide open for anything and anyone to come in.

Then there were severe earthquakes, the rocks tore, and the graves opened, where many bodies of the saints were uncovered. They arose from the dead and went into Jerusalem where they were seen by many according to Matthew 27:53.

> Just before the veil rent Jesus said, "IT IS FINISHED." What is finished? All that it took for the forgiveness of man's sins.

Now this scene took place over 2,000 years ago. What happened to the daily sacrifices from that point on the scriptures don't tell us. But the Jews did not accept the spotless Lamb of God, as the one-time sacrifice; they perhaps went together, maybe they had a work bee, I don't know, and perhaps they started sewing the torn curtain back together again, so they could resume their lifeless, unacceptable sacrifices again.

Now, let's back up and look at some of these happenings more closely.

Just before the veil rent Jesus said, "IT IS FINISHED." And when He said that the veil rent. What did He mean by these words? What is finished?

All the work that the Father had sent Him to do. All that was necessary for the salvation of man; all that it took for the forgiveness of man's sins, and all that it took to deliver man from the power of sin. It is finished!

In German the words "It is finished," mean it is fully accomplished. "Es ist vollbracht."

It was a fulfillment of the prophecy of Genesis 3:15: The woman's seed will bruise the serpent's head.

According to our text immediately after Jesus said, "It is finished," and died, the veil rent. Why did the veil tear? And what was its purpose?

The death of Christ related to the rending of the veil. The death of Christ. When he said, "It is finished," He bowed His head and gave up the ghost and immediately the veil tore.

The veil is a huge, heavy curtain. According to the Old Testament this curtain was made of badger skins, that hung as a wall, separating the Holiest of Holies from the rest of the temple.

It took many, many lives for that curtain to be made. Lives of badgers. I don't know how many— some students say that veil could have been as thick as three feet.

I don't know. But all of you know this: tearing leather isn't easy. It has no grain. It's not like a piece of cloth that you start with scissors and it tears straight.

No, leather tears hard. And this curtain—you

probably could have hooked two big tractors to it and couldn't have pulled it apart.

There was no mistake to it. God's hand was in it. And it didn't tear from the bottom up—it tore from the top down. Again a mystery.

Behind that veil was the ark of the covenant containing Aaron's budded rod, manna saved from the wilderness, and stone tables containing the Ten Commandments. That was behind that veil.

But the most significant was the mercy seat on top of the ark of the covenant in between the two cherubims. The mercy seat, that's where God said He would dwell in David's time—God said, "I will dwell between the cherubims on the mercy seat, that's where I will dwell."

This was an extremely holy, sacred place, where only the high priest was allowed to enter.

At Christ's death, when the veil was rent and opened up the Holiest of Holies for all, it was the end of all earthly high priests. All animal sacrifices for man's sins were finished.

Jesus had become the Lamb of God which taketh away the sins of the world. A fulfillment of all prior animal sacrifices—all these pointed to a single sacrifice.

Jesus Christ! When He bowed His head, God

> God looked upon the travail of His Son's soul and the scriptures tell me He was satisfied. Let's be careful that we are not dissatisfied.

made it evident to everyone that the temple is useless. It's past. No more sacrifices. No more high priests, taking the sins of the people before God.

God looked down and watched His Son being crucified, and I believe the heart of God… How would it be for you fathers—if we'd have to stand and watch our only son be crucified by cruel men and we'd know we had all the power to simply squash everything that was taking place?

And we'd just watch it. And then hear our own son cry out in agony, "Dad, why have you left me?"

God looked upon the travail of His Son's soul and the scriptures tell me He was satisfied.

Let's be careful that we are not dissatisfied. God was satisfied, and the rending of the veil was proof. Full payment was made for the sins of man, and the rending of the veil was God's stamp of approval which read: "Paid in full by the blood of the Lamb."

There was a time in my Christian life when I wondered why God is so hard on someone who won't accept what He says.

In Revelation it tells us that the fearful shall have their part in the lake of fire. The Hebrew writer says,

If any man draw back—this is God speaking—*my soul shall have no pleasure in him.*

I used to think, *But surely, God, evil people that have evil intentions: man slayers—woman slayers—child molest-*

The Hebrew writer says, If any man draw back—This is God speaking—*my soul shall have no pleasure in him.*

ers, murderers, anything evil you can think of; there are men in this world that are going to hell because of that. Is it really fair, God, to send someone to the same place that was just too fearful to accept what you said?

And the fearful shall have their part in the lake of fire with the devil and the beast. Who are the fearful?

People who won't accept what God has said, afraid to commit themselves to it. It's unbelief. *Take heed, brethren, lest there be in any of you an evil heart of unbelief, in departing from the living God.*

When God went to that extreme, paid the debt of our sins, and when man refuses to accept that God said, "I'm satisfied," that's a slap in God's face.

The rending of the veil was God's invitation to all kindreds, nations, tongues and people, to come and communicate with Him.

Who are the fearful? People who won't accept what God has said—that's unbelief.

Though your sins be as scarlet, they shall be white as snow.

Though they be as crimson, they shall be as wool.

At the rending of the veil, the mercy seat opened wide and Jesus Christ, not some mere earthly man, sits within the veil waiting for all who are weary and heavy laden to give rest to their weary souls. "Come unto me." *Kommet her zu mir alle, die ihr mühselig und belauden seid; ich will euch erquicken. Nihmet auf mein Joch und lernet von mir; denn ich bin sanftmütig und von Herzen demütig; so werdet ihr Ruhe finden für eure Seelen.* (Matthew 11:28,29).

What am I talking about when I use these terms of speech? When Satan tried to eliminate Christ by crucifying Him he had no idea what his actions would accomplish. All he could think in his rage was: "Get rid of Christ. Get rid of Him, in any way that I can, wipe Him off the face of the earth." But God is over all, and God used his very plans to bring about his undoing.

He had no idea that the death of Christ which he hungrily sought after would be the very undoing of his own power and plans. He had no idea he was playing right into God's plan of salvation and getting his own head stepped on in the process. He had no idea that evil intent and actions would open the way into the Holiest of Holies, and would open up the way for all his prisoners to escape. Hallelujah!

I Cor. 2:7-8 speaks of God's wisdom, and how the

princes of this world didn't understand or know this wisdom or they would not have crucified Christ.

The princes of this world were getting their orders from the devil to crucify the Christ, because he did not understand what that would accomplish.

But, beloved, after the devil saw his own mistake he tried, and he still tries to this day, to cover up his tracks with lies. The devil has nothing left but lies. He is defeated!

The majority of mankind believe those lies, and it comes a lot closer than we think.

The devil knows he is defeated, but he uses lies to cover up. He continues to use people's emotions to undermine their faith and paralyze them with doubts.

He establishes in millions of people doctrines and beliefs that have no scriptural foundation whatsoever, contrary to the finished work on the cross.

Yet people hang onto these false beliefs and preach them across thousands of pulpits, ensnaring millions that truth could liberate.

Satan could not stop the rending of the veil, giving free access to all to boldly come to the throne of grace. Satan could not stop that.

And so with lies he has succeeded in employing thousands of people to work together to <u>mend the veil</u>. Sew it back together again. The irony and

> *S*atan could not stop the rending of the veil, giving free access to all to boldly come to the throne of grace... And so with lies he has succeeded in employing thousands of people to work together to <u>mend the veil</u>.

the deception is that most people employed in mending the veil don't realize who they are working for.

They think they are preaching truth and serving God. They are sincere in their belief and have no idea that if they'd hold up their belief to the scriptures it wouldn't hold any water; it's so full of holes.

Now, I want to define the mending of the curtain. Mending the curtain is anything that obscures or hinders free access to the mercy seat and throne of God. It involves anything that adds to or takes away from the simplicity of the gospel and what Jesus said is finished.

Anyone who believes or teaches anything but true liberty in Jesus alone is employed in this mending of the veil whether he realizes it or not.

A lot of Christian preachers make the gospel so difficult, so hard to accept, that being accepted by God becomes such an issue that many find it hard to honestly sing, "Blessed assurance, Jesus is mine." It's crippling the churches.

I'm reminded of Paul's words to the Corinthians: "I fear." Nearly 2,000 years ago when Paul wrote the epistles he already feared. He said, *I fear, lest the subtlety of the devil comes among you and destroys the simplicity that is in Christ Jesus.* (II Corinthians 11:3).

Paul talks about a corrupted mind: the simple gospel is not believed. Since the veil was rent, the devil has been feverishly trying to mend it back again.

He desperately doesn't want men to know the truth and find freedom. Satan has removed the truth, and people are too ignorant to know and believe in the rent veil, let alone the mending of it.

These would include the religions of Hinduism, Buddhism, Islam and many more religions. But many more religions come closer to Christianity.

> Anyone who believes or teaches anything but true liberty in Jesus alone is employed in this mending of the veil whether he realizes it or not.

Take Catholicism for instance. The Roman Catholic gospel denies that Christ's sacrifice was sufficient. Don't let anyone fool you on that. The priesthood re-sacrifices Christ again in their sacrifice of the mass.

I have read Catholic laws. A Catholic is anathematized, he is disowned, kicked out of the church, if he dares to say that he knows he is saved.

It comes a lot closer home than we think. The Catholic is anathematized if he says that the sacrifice of Christ was sufficient for the forgiveness of sins. He is anathematized if he denies that the mass is an ongoing sacrifice to be offered for the living and the dead.

Can we see how the devil has succeeded in getting descendants of the Anabaptists to revert to the religious beliefs their forefathers came out of? With seeds of doubt he succeeds in bringing into bondage the descendants of those that were at one time set free.

To the simplicity of the gospel, Rome Catholicism has added baptism, good works, penance, prayers to Mary and the saints, suffering in purgatory, mass for the dead—to get them out of purgatory, last rites called extreme unction, holy water, candles, rituals and the list goes on.

These are all extensions and all add to—to <u>what is finished</u>.

It didn't stop with the Catholics. Some of our forefathers were burned at the stake for standing against these things. Today their descendants are back to base one. Anyone that is involved in these is complicating the gospel's simplicity and is employed in mending the curtain again.

Sin has always been present since the fall of man. Mending the veil goes back to the beginning of the

The Faith That Overcomes

church. Who can deny its existence in the epistles? You'll find it there in the early church, curtain menders.

Some of the Galatians allowed themselves to be bewitched into this mending process by demanding circumcision in addition to grace alone.

Grace by faith. Paul spent the greater portion of his epistle to the Colossians to convince them against this mending of the veil.

He had great fears that men would beguile them with enticing words. He warned them and told them to be aware, to be alert, lest any man spoil them; that means to rob them from the simplicity of the gospel through philosophy and vain deceit after the traditions of men, after the rudiments of the world, the high-sounding nonsense of man, and not after Christ.

He tried to point them alone to Christ. He said it's Christ plus nothing. He said, _In Him dwelleth all the fulness of the Godhead_.

He said, "Ye are complete in Him. You don't need to add anything." Paul went on to say in Chapter 2: "You've been buried with Christ in baptism, wherein also ye are risen with Him through the faith of the operation of God, who has raised Him from the dead."

He said, _"And you, being dead in your sins and the_

uncircumcision of your flesh, has (past tense) *He quickened together with Him, having forgiven all your trespasses, blotting out the handwriting of ordinances that was against us, which was contrary to us, and took it out of the way, nailing them to the cross."*

Paul is saying you died. The old man died with Christ, was buried with Christ in baptism, arose with Christ in newness of life. Paul is saying, "You were part of that finished work and were resurrected within the rent veil."

Paul continues on in verse 20, with the question, Why? "Why then if ye are dead with Christ and have been set free, why, as though this didn't happen, are you again bringing yourselves back into bondage with all kinds of ordinances of touch not, taste not, handle not?"

He said, "Ye are complete in Him. You don't need to add anything."

Why are you living as though it wasn't finished and the veil isn't rent? Why are you trying to sew it back together again?

In many epistles you'll find curtain menders. Paul was greatly concerned and repeatedly warned against it. Peter talks about those who are blind and cannot see afar off, and have forgotten that they were purged from their sins.

How do we forget so easily? We get occupied

with less important things and soon we are influenced by curtain menders.

It doesn't take long for us to fall back into this performance, acceptance mentality. It doesn't take long at all.

John, in his epistles, makes sure that the child of God knows where He

> Peter talks about those who are blind and cannot see afar off, and have forgotten that they were purged from their sins.

stands concerning his salvation and his relationship with God. I believe John had a real burden for that. I don't believe any epistle makes it clearer than John.

Usually when someone gets saved, we tell him, "Read the epistles of John." He says in his epistles in different places, "These things have I written unto you, so that you may know—hereby we know that He abideth in us by the Spirit which He hath given us." John was concerned about the believer's assurance and how important it is. He knew the importance of the rent veil.

Satan not only lies to receptive hearts to create blindness toward the rent veil, or obscure the open way to the throne of grace, but he incorporates false beliefs and counterfeit religions. He tries to counterfeit the true source of peace and security.

He uses the weak in faith to mend the veil and

that should not surprise us. There's nothing harder in the Christian life than to maintain the faith.

Nothing. It goes against everything that is natural. It goes against everything that is tangible and temporal. It militates against our five senses and it must continue to exist without physical evidence.

We need to bring this closer home and make some applications. Where are we at in what we believe? Are we free?

How do we look at the finished work of Christ?

How do we view the rent veil? What is our understanding of it? What are we believing and teaching concerning this? I believe a lot of false teaching is going on that is not liberating people, but rather holding them in bondage. They are held in bondage by their emotions and this performance, acceptance mentality.

> There's nothing harder in the Christian life than to maintain the faith.

If they perform well, they feel accepted, if they don't, they feel rejected, and some of the teachings and writings in our day encourage this.

The question this afternoon is: Do I really believe the words of Jesus?

It is finished.

If I do, then I will understand the rent veil and come boldly to the throne of grace. If I don't, then I will be held in bondage of unbelief and the rent veil will not mean a whole lot to me, because I believe the travail of my own soul must be involved to gain recognition and merit.

Listen, if we want to be blessed and encouraged in our Christian walk, and not be mending the veil, we need to clearly understand two foundational areas that relate to our salvation: justification and sanctification.

Maybe it's getting old to you, the four messages that we've been preaching, but it's very important that we have line upon line, precept upon precept, here a little and there a little, until we get it.

Whether or not we will have victory in our Christian life depends on how we relate to these two: justification and sanctification. Justification is positional; a state of being. A place we stand by faith. Romans 5:2.

It is obtained by faith. *Therefore being justified by faith we have peace with God through our Lord Jesus Christ* (Romans 5:1).

Justification is a position in Christ to where it's just as if I had not sinned. Romans 4:25 says: Jesus Christ was delivered unto death for our offenses, our sins, and was raised again for our justification. He was raised from the dead so we could be put into a state of being just as if we had not sinned, so He could intercede for us to the Father and present us with Him to the Father, just as if we had not sinned. This is what it means to be justified.

> *Justification is a position in Christ to where it's just as if I had not sinned.*

For most of us this is not hard to accept by faith. We believe this, and at least partially understand it.

When it comes to sanctification, then I'm afraid that many of God's children are not clear. Because of this, unscriptural teaching goes on, which confuses people. This produces defeat and no real power over sin.

The church today has a weakness in lifting some historical writer on a stage—almost worshiping him because of some books he wrote. But if they had lived in his day, they probably would not have agreed with him. We should be very careful with that.

Some of the men that are quoted behind pulpits we would not agree with if they would live today.

I urge you to jot down scriptures as we go through this subject and take them home and be Bereans.

To many Christians sanctification means a state or condition reached through a process of diligently seeking God through prayer, meditation, and Bible reading. You've heard many times: progressive sanctification.

<u>That's not scriptural</u>.

I'm talking about Bible sanctification. I understand some people look at sanctification as being set apart for the work of God.

They use progressive sanctification. They think a person set apart for God's work progresses in usefulness in God's Kingdom and progresses in his sanctification.

Now if that is your definition of sanctification, then I'm not going to quarrel with you. But that's not Bible sanctification. We'd better be careful how we use that word, because sanctification is not a process.

Christian growth is. I'll explain. I want to be understood correctly. Many people believe that sanctification comes through diligently seeking God through prayer, meditation, and Bible reading. They look at sanctification as the effect of seeking God, but it's the total opposite. Sanctification is the cause—the effect is prayer, seeking God on a deeper level, etc. That's the effect of sanctification, not the cause of it.

I'm preaching to converted people. These messages are not for the sinner.

I do not find scriptures to support the teaching that sanctification is a progressive work, even though I at one time felt that way and taught it. But search the scriptures. You will not find sanctification as a process.

Sanctification is a state of being. In short, it's the state of being holy. Look up the word sanctification in any dictionary or Bible dictionary.

My dictionary was written in the 1800s and I like it because more liberal terms were not used. But the definition of sanctification is a state of being holy.

The dictionary gives it: made holy; made free from sin. There are no degrees of sanctification any more than there are degrees of holiness.

Maybe we need to talk about that, too. There are no degrees of holiness recorded in the Bible. Do you believe that?

<u>That surprised me</u>. I got my concordance and searched the scriptures; I was sure there are degrees of holiness. There are no degrees of holiness written in the Bible as far as a person is concerned.

The word "holiest" is recorded three times in the Bible, and all three times it's referring to the mercy seat of God, which means God is holiest. I have no qualms with that. God is holiest.

And the word "holier" is recorded once. Listen to this: And God rebuked the children of Israel because they didn't see their backslidden condition and considered themselves holier than other people.

Everywhere else in the Bible from cover to cover the word is always used in the singular sense: holy.

I know people sometimes say these people are holier than others and they are the holiest of the holy, but those are man's terms, not God's terms. God does not see it that way; that's only man's judgment. If holiness or sanctification could be obtained by levels or degrees, how would you obtain it?

You say, "I'm converted; I was saved by grace through faith; I'm washed in the blood of Jesus. I was made holy." How are you going to get holier? Think about that.

First we think that if I live a certain way…if I do this—you're going back to works.

If holiness could be attained by more submission or more concentration or yielding of ourselves a living sacrifice, then holiness or sanctification could be obtained by our works. There are no degrees of sanctification or holiness.

If a person is holy, then he is holy. He can't be made holier. The Bible teaches: growing in grace and knowledge, but I don't find growing in holiness.

> There are no degrees of holiness written in the Bible as far as a person is concerned.

The same is true with sanctification. If we are sanctified, then we are made holy. We can't be more sanctified. We need to distinguish between sanctification and Christian growth or maturity.

Take Job for instance. I'll use a little illustration

> *If holiness could be attained by more submission or more concentration or yielding of ourselves a living sacrifice, then holiness or sanctification could be obtained by our works.*

here. Was Job holy? Absolutely. Job was holy. Was he sanctified? Of course, he was sanctified. God said that he was a perfect and upright man.

Did Job need maturity? Absolutely. Even though in the process of maturing, he never charged God foolishly, the Bible tells us. He was holy through it all, yet he came out of his sufferings a changed man.

His testimony before he entered that suffering was: "I have heard by the hearing of the ear," and his testimony when he came out of it was, "Now I have seen Him and I abhor myself and repent in dust and ashes."

What happened to Job? Was he more holy through the process?

No. But <u>he matured</u>.

Think of a green apple growing on a tree. In the spring, blossoms appear on an apple tree and after a few weeks, if you observe closely, there's a very little apple in place of the blossom.

That little green apple may be just as big as your fingernail. It's perfect. It's perfect, but it's not ripe.

Wait two months and that apple is big, nice… perfect, in its stage of growth. But it's not ripe.

You get what I'm saying? That's how the Christian is. When you are born again—when you, by the blood of the Lord Jesus Christ, are washed of your sins, you are made holy.

You can mature. You can grow. That's all a process, but you're not going to get holier.

The person that was lost in the gutters of sin and got saved is as acceptable to God as a saint who has been walking with God for fifty years.

I praise God for that, because I have a lot of growing to do. And if I would gauge my holiness or my acceptance with God according to my Christian growth, I wouldn't rank very high.

When Jesus said in Matthew: *"Be ye perfect, even as my Father in heaven is perfect,"* He was not talking about a level of perfection, but a state of perfection.

He, who knew no sin, was made sin for us, so that we could be made the righteousness of God in Him. That simply is saying: He, Jesus Christ, who knew no sin, was made sin instead of us, so that we could be made as righteous as God in Him. That's all that's saying. It's not a process. It's a state of being.

If we don't keep this straight and if we believe that we'll progress in our sanctification, we'll believe like the Galatians. Begin in the Spirit, but made perfect in the flesh. In other words, born again by the power of God through the Holy Spirit, but sanctified by my efforts of cleaning up my life. The more I clean myself the holier I get. There wouldn't be a whole lot of chance for somebody like me if that was true. Justified by faith, but sanctified by works.

II Thessalonians 2:13 teaches that we are sanctified by the Spirit by believing the truth. If we don't keep these things straight, we will soon believe that adding to our faith: virtue, temperance, patience, godliness, brotherly kindness and charity is progressive sanctification, instead of Christian growth.

We would look at one Christian as being more holy than another, instead of more mature. Hebrews 2:11 says: *Both He that sanctifies and they who are sanctified are all of one: for which cause He is not ashamed to call them brethren.* That has such depth to it.

> The person that was lost in the gutters of sin and got saved is as acceptable to God as a saint who has been walking with God for fifty years.

The reason that Jesus Christ is not ashamed to call us brethren is because we are as sanctified as He. And listen! If there were degrees of sanctification or holiness, then Jesus Christ would be more ashamed of me than somebody else.

No. That's not the way it is. He accepts us all as sanctified if we're truly washed in the blood of Jesus.

We have been made holy. Again, this message is not to the sinner or someone who is out there trying to get away with something and not willing to repent.

Christian maturity is what determines usefulness in God's Kingdom—not degrees of holiness.

> If there were degrees of sanctification or holiness, then Jesus Christ would be more ashamed of me than somebody else.

In Acts chapter 6 they chose seven men full of the Holy Ghost. What are they talking about? Men full of the Holy Ghost. What is the Holy Ghost? It's a person of the Godhead. Did they have more of the Holy Ghost than the rest?

Or did Jesus Christ or the Holy Ghost have more of them than the rest? Were they more sanctified—holier than the rest? Or was their usefulness determined by their maturity?

They were selected because they were more mature than others. A person's maturity is determined by his faith. There's no question.

That's why God could say, "Go to a child, learn, and receive that childlike faith."

Some of our learning has taken us farther away from God rather than closer. A person's usefulness in the Kingdom of God is in direct proportion to how he accepts by faith God's acceptance of him.

I'm going to repeat that because it is vital to remember. A person's usefulness in the Kingdom of God is in direct proportion to how he accepts by faith God's acceptance of him.

> *Some of our learning has taken us farther away from God rather than closer.*

Until we fully accept and believe that it is finished and we are accepted in the beloved, we will not have joy, peace, or love, etc. Without that, we are not very useful in the Kingdom of God.

So, how are we sanctified? How are we made holy? By Jesus Christ alone according to I Corinthians 1:30—*Jesus, who of God is made unto us wisdom, righteousness, sanctification, and redemption!*

Many Christians mistake the separating of sanctification from justification as the source of power. They think that sanctification is experience apart from the cross where justification was found. But Paul sets us straight in Col. 2:6: *As ye have therefore received Christ Jesus the Lord, so walk ye in Him.*

At the same place you met Jesus for your justification, there you need to go for your sanctification.

In other words, the same power needed for the one is needed for the other, at the same place: the cross. The cross that justifies is also the cross that sanctifies.

Faith in Christ's death on the cross for our sins justifies us; faith in our death with Christ upon the same cross sanctifies us. Faith in Christ's death saves us from the punishment of our past sins; faith in our death, death to the old man, saves us from the power of present sins.

Romans 6:6 says: *Knowing this, that our old man is crucified with Him, that the body of sin might be destroyed, that henceforth we should not serve sin. 7 For he that is dead is freed from sin.*

That is what you call sanctification: being delivered from sin's power.

The rent veil freely opens the way to the cross, and anytime we find ourselves seeking another way for victory we are mending the veil.

Remember, it's not what you do for God that sanctifies you. Most Christians don't have a problem with that, but listen. Neither is it what God does through you that sanctifies you. It's what God has already done to you: 2,000 years ago He crucified you with Christ.

Romans 6 is on sanctification (not justification), that we sin not. *Shall we continue in sin, that grace may abound?* The whole chapter is written so that we sin not, how to be freed from sin's power, and how this is done by reckoning ourselves dead unto sin and alive unto God.

Just as we look back 2,000 years ago to Christ's death for justification, so we need to, by faith, go to the crucifixion of the old man with Christ for our sanctification.

A lot of Christian writers… I don't want you to write these men off. But I have checked their articles and I have read their books and I'm not judging these men; I'm just telling you. <u>Beware!</u> They have a lot of good writing. But there's also some writing there that's questionable.

Like I said, "I'm not judging these men." I want that clear, but I could not believe when I read the book on Absolute Surrender. He believed the Christian walk is Romans 7 from beginning to end.

I have all these books, and much of that writing is an attempt to daily crucify the old man, instead of reckoning him already dead as Romans 6 tells us. It's what you call principle sanctification rather than sanctification by faith.

If you totally surrender, crucify yourself every day, pray for hours each day, then eventually as you get old…maybe 40 years down the road and you're white, and gray-haired, you can expect to be sanctified. That's heresy.

If you're not sanctified today, you're not ready to

die.

I'm not belittling reading the Word and praying, but they need to be the result of sanctification, not the means of it.

When Jesus spoke about daily taking up His cross and following Him, He was talking about physical death; many are put to death for their faith. It's going on right now in many countries around the world. In every one of the gospels where Jesus speaks of this, it's in the context of physical suffering for the gospel's sake.

If Jesus would have meant to daily take up

> If you're not sanctified today, you're not ready to die.

our cross and daily crucify the old man, He would have contradicted Paul who said three times in the scriptures that the old man is already dead.

What about Paul saying, "I die daily"?

Check it out for yourselves. Everywhere that Paul talks about these things, it's about the physical. Man misinterprets the Bible so that the gospel is no longer simple. Someone asked Martin Luther if he feels God has accepted him and he said, "No. But I stand on facts, not my feelings."

If you struggle continuously with feeling accepted, distinguish between God's acceptance and the feelings. I want you to remember this: those who continually struggle with feeling accepted by God have to distinguish between God's acceptance and the feelings. Don't get them mixed up.

If you have accepted that God loves you, then you will be affected by it, but don't go by your emotions to see whether or not you are accepted.

Parents trying to guide youth to victory, pastors and teachers trying to direct the church, and counselors, we need answers for the defeated lives among God's people. We need to believe and preach a gospel that delivers and works.

The way is open and we need to meditate on the words of Jesus, "It is finished." We need to pray for discernment and a deeper faith lest we be found working with the multitudes in mending the veil. Hebrews 10:17 says:

> *We need to believe and preach a gospel that delivers and works.*

And their sins and iniquities will I remember no more. Verses 19-23: *Having therefore, brethren, boldness to enter into the holiest by the blood of Jesus, 20. By a new and living way, which He hath consecrated for us, through the veil, that is to say, His flesh; 21. And having an high priest over the house of God; 22. Let us draw near with a true heart in full assurance of faith, having our hearts sprinkled from an evil conscience, and our bodies washed with*

*pure water. 23. Let us hold fast the profession of
our faith without wavering; (for He is faithful that
promised;)*

Hebrews 4:16: *Let us therefore come boldly unto
the throne of grace, that we may obtain mercy, and
find grace to help in time of need.*

Let's pray. "Oh, Father, I pray that these truths
would sink deep down in our hearts. I pray, Lord,
that we would be set free. Not free to serve the flesh,
but free to serve You with an open conscience.

We don't want the flesh, Father. We know that is
only bondage. I pray, Father, that Your Word would
continue to liberate Your people. And I pray, Father,
for Your ministers of the gospel. That they with holy
boldness would be willing to preach the truth in love.
And, Father, I pray that You would bless these people
here as they go to their homes after this weekend.

I pray, Father, that a newfound liberty could be
theirs, and that they could experience the power of
God in their lives. Daily, hourly, moment by moment
the surging power of the Holy Spirit in their lives,
Lord, to where they don't even want to do evil things.
They are so thoroughly delivered. Their whole Christian
life which has been a "have-to," is now a "get-to."

Bless us, Lord. Only You can do this, and we
commit these services, these meetings, into Your

hands, Lord, for Your glory and for Your praise, Father. In Jesus' name I pray these things. Amen.

We're going to have our family come up and sing. The song is on page 49.

Praise God!

Hallelujah!